ANGELS OF GOD

Angels of God

The Bible, The Church and the Heavenly Hosts

Mike Aquilina

SERVANT BOOKS

PUBLISHED BY ST. ANTHONY MESSENGER PRESS
CINCINNATI, OHIO

Excerpts from *The Fathers of the Church: Expanded Edition,* by Mike Aquilina, copyright ©2006 by Our Sunday Visitor, are used by permission of Our Sunday Visitor.

Unless otherwise noted, Scripture passages have been taken from the *Revised Standard Version,* Catholic edition. Copyright © 1946, 1952, 1971 by the Division of Christian Education of the National Council of Churches of Christ in the USA. Used by permission. All rights reserved.
Note: The editors of this volume have made minor changes in capitalization to some of the Scripture quotations herein. Please consult the original source for proper capitalization.

Cover and book design by Mark Sullivan
Cover image: Angelico, Fra (1387-1455). Detail of Angel Annunciate from the Polyptych of the Dominicans. Galleria Nazionale dell'Umbria, Perugia, Italy. Photo credit: Scala/Art Resource, NY

LIBRARY OF CONGRESS CATALOGING-IN-PUBLICATION DATA
Aquilina, Mike.
Angels of God : the Bible, the church, and the heavenly hosts / Mike Aquilina.
p. cm.
Includes bibliographical references.
ISBN 978-0-86716-898-3 (pbk. : alk. paper) 1. Angels. I. Title.
BT966.3.A68 2009
235'.3—dc22
2008056005

ISBN 978-0-86716-898-3

Published by Servant Books, an imprint of St. Anthony Messenger Press
28 W. Liberty St.
Cincinnati, OH 45202
www.AmericanCatholic.org
www.ServantBooks.org

Printed in the United States of America.

Printed on acid-free paper.

10 11 12 13 6 5 4 3

For Grace Marie

Contents

Acknowledgments

. . . .

Never before have I called upon heaven so much in the preparation of a book, so I would be remiss if I failed to acknowledge the assistance of the angels. If there are errors in the book, I take the blame for not listening well enough.

I'm also deeply indebted to several of the sainted ancients, especially Pope Saint Gregory the Great and the author best known as Saint Denis or "Dionysius the Areopagite." Their classic angelologies are mind-blowing. Several of their works are available only in nineteenth-century translations that are difficult for modern Americans to read with understanding. (The English language has undergone great changes in two hundred years.) So I have adapted the material, translating it from Victorian English to modern English, consulting the Greek or Latin originals whenever possible.

The main series of translations from which I've drawn are the *Ante-Nicene Fathers* and the *Nicene and Post-Nicene Fathers*, series one and two. All three series are available many places online: You'll find them at www.ccel.org with page numbers intact and at www.NewAdvent.org in plain text. A multivolume reprint edition is available from Hendrickson Publishers in Peabody, Massachusetts.

I'm grateful to my colleagues, especially to Chris Bailey—who is a dear friend, sometime coauthor, candid critic, brilliant translator and the best editor I know—but also to Scott Hahn,

David Scott and Rob Corzine, who encouraged me mightily and helped me, as always, to find the most perfect sources in the most hidden corners of the world's libraries. My two favorite hagiologists, Maureen O'Brien and Matthew Bunson, answered some key questions and patiently guided me to ancient and medieval source texts.

My editor, Cindy Cavnar, thought up this book in the first place and insisted that I write it. She is an actual grace in my life.

The poet Coventry Patmore often wrote about his wife; and when he did he portrayed her as an image of the angels:

> And, when we knelt, she seem'd to be
> An angel teaching me to pray.[1]

If I were a poet, I would write something like that for my wife, Terri, who inspires whatever good I do.

 THE EVERYWHERE OF ANGELS

Angels are everywhere!

So proclaims the sweatshirt of the lady who gives me Communion when I go to Mass at a parish near my home. The shirt is oversized, sky blue, with a flock of Victorian angels flitting about the ornate, glittery lettering of the message.

There was a time in my life when I would have found every detail of that shirt annoying—from the depiction of the angels, who look a lot like the sugarplum fairies in my kids' storybooks, to the exclamation point at the end of the slogan, which violates my every sense of journalistic and theological decorum. But now, for me, that shirt is a prayer. And this book is, in a sense, an *amen*, my confession of faith.

How did I get from there to here? It's a difficult story to tell, and I'll come to it in a minute.

Our first order of business, though, should be that slogan: *Angels are everywhere!*

Indeed they are. And I'm not talking just about their commercial exploitation. Yes, we've survived the decades when pop culture felt it necessary to remind us that angels were not only "in America" but also "in the architecture" and even "in the outfield." One author claimed that 10 percent of all popular songs of the 1950s–1980s mentioned angels. I haven't checked the *Billboard* charts myself, but I find no reason to doubt his point. In my childhood home the radio was always on, and I thank God I had catechism classes to offset the strange theological suggestions of titles like "Earth Angel," "Teen Angel," "Angel Baby" and "Undercover Angel," not to mention the dubious metaphysics of "Heaven Must Be Missing an Angel."

Angels are everywhere in film and music, and that alone can be a turnoff. Hollywood tends to trivialize angels the way it trivializes sex, reducing something profoundly spiritual to a mere curiosity before mass-producing it into an inescapable nuisance —as irritating as an unforgettable advertising jingle. Our temptation is to lose interest in the subject entirely, to dismiss the study of angels as a pastime of flakey New Age types or very sweet coworkers who also collect unicorns and rainbow sun catchers. It's then that we wince at the sight of an "Angels are everywhere!" sweatshirt.

But we mustn't allow Hollywood and Madison Avenue to win in this way. I say this not because angels are sensitive beings who will be hurt by our ingratitude but because angels are a large part of reality and, as with other large parts of reality—speeding Mack trucks, for example, or looming brick walls—we benefit greatly from their service, and we ignore them at our peril.

The truth is that angels *are* everywhere, and I'd like us to spend this book pondering the many ways that statement is true. First, though, let's consider some that should be obvious to us but perhaps are not.

Angels are everywhere in Scripture. We find angels from the first pages of Genesis to the last pages of Revelation, and not just as bit players. They play crucial roles in the drama of our creation, fall and salvation.

In the beginning it is a fallen angel, in the form of a serpent, who tempts Adam and Eve. When our first parents are expelled from the Garden, God places angels at the entryway as a sign of judgment. It is an angel who stays the hand of Abraham when he is about to sacrifice Isaac. Angels watch over Moses and the Israelites as they make their exodus from Egypt and as they receive the law from God. Angels minister at the temple of Solomon. Angels deliver the word of the Lord to the prophets.

The trend continues through the New Testament. Angels announce the conception and birth of Jesus and of John the Baptist. Angels guide all sorts of people to worship at the crib of Jesus. Angels guide the Holy Family away from imminent danger. Angels minister to Jesus when he's fasting in the desert and when he's suffering in the garden. Angels watch at his empty tomb and accompany him at his ascension, announcing his glory as at his birth. Angels accompany the apostles as they establish the Church of Christ. The book of Revelation and the Letter to the Hebrews show us that angels are continually at work in our Church and in our world.

Angels are everywhere in our prayer. In the Mass two of the most beloved prayers are songs that, according to Scripture, mankind learned from the angels: the *Gloria* (Luke 2:13–14: "Glory to God in the highest!") and the *Sanctus* (Isaiah 6:2–3: "Holy, holy, holy!"). The Church often invokes the heavenly host at the Preface of the Eucharistic Prayer: "And so, with all the choirs of angels in heaven / we proclaim your glory / and join in their unending hymn of praise."[1] In the great prayer itself, the priest asks God that "your angel may take this sacrifice / to your altar in heaven."[2]

And angelic prayer is hardly something we reserve for Sunday Mass. Catholics imitate and invoke the angels in many of the devotions that have been popular through the centuries. When we pray the Hail Mary, we are praying the words that the angel spoke to the Blessed Virgin, as they are recorded in Saint Luke's Gospel (see Luke 1:28). When we offer the traditional noontime prayer, the *Angelus*, we recall that very story of the Annunciation to Mary. For more than a century now, the popes have encouraged recitation of certain prayers to Saint Michael the Archangel.

Angels are everywhere in Scripture, everywhere in our Christian worship, everywhere in sacred Tradition. We find them there at the heart of the faith, attending to the Holy Trinity and the Holy Family and to us. That's the place that God gave them in divine revelation. That's the place that Jesus gave them in his preaching and earthly life. If we relegate them to the periphery, we are distorting the faith, for we are not living it as we received it but as we prefer it to be. If we are ashamed of the angels who love us and serve us—and whom God has given to us!—should we not expect them to be ashamed of us at our judgment?

The story of the angels did not come to an end as John wrote the last words of the book of Revelation. Their mission and ministry go on. Whether we acknowledge them or not, these mysterious creatures are omnipresent in our lives, from the first moments of our conception to our last ebbing breath. They are active in our prayer, in our choices, in the order of the Church and in the order of our world. And as in the Bible, so in our lives, they are not bit players. They play crucial roles in our personal dramas.

Angelic Encounters

I confess, though, that I did not always give them their due. Not so long ago I kept the angels on a remote reservation in my spiritual life. I would never deny their existence, because I knew that the doctrine of angels was well established in Tradition and nonnegotiable. But I wanted to make sure that no one suspected *me* of trafficking with the angels of pop culture (and some popular devotion). It hardly seemed intelligent—and it certainly seemed unmanly—to be hanging around with Victorian sprites and cherubic fairies.

Then something happened. Two close friends of mine—a man and a woman, both of them models of Christian life for me—were diagnosed with terminal cancer. As their diseases progressed, I spent countless hours with them, first on drives to chemo and in waiting rooms, then in hospital suites and finally at bedside vigils.

And I noticed something. As their bodies wasted away, both friends began to mention the angels more often in conversation. It was all very casual, as if angelic presence was as ordinary a topic as eating lunch or paying the electric bill.

I wondered why, back then, and I still do. As I reflect on the experience, it occurs to me that angels are like us in some ways and unlike us in other, very important ways. They are persons, just as we are, and so they are conscious and capable of love and moral choice. Unlike us, however, the angels are pure spirits. We humans are spiritual beings but not *exclusively* spiritual. We are composite, made up of a spiritual soul and a material body. Death comes for us when the soul is separated from the body. As that separation is imminent, at least for devout souls, our own "spirituality" must become more evident, and so our kinship with the angels.

As my friends entered the last stages of cancer, and even as they drifted from consciousness, invocations of the angels, especially Saint Michael, came more frequently to their lips. Death is never pretty, but bodily suffering is only part of the trial and is sometimes accompanied by tremendous spiritual struggle—spiritual warfare. It became clear to me, through the witness of my friends, that the angels are indeed fighting beside us in these battles.

Reflecting a bit further, I recognized that the battle is not reserved for the end of earthly life. It's raging now. You and I are the battleground, and we are the spoils of war. For us to ignore the angels would be a sign not only of disordered pride but of colossal stupidity.

Why did God make angels?

One reason appears to be that they are our guardians and guides. Even though they are far stronger than we are and far more intelligent than we are, they live to serve us. By their ministry to you and me, they give glory to almighty God. For us to refuse such service would be a sign, again, not just of disordered pride but of sheer madness.

After all, *angels are everywhere!* And our fellowship with them is not an ornament on our religion; it's a life skill.

In the following chapters I'll take a closer look at the evidence of angelic activity in our lives. There are many different ways to approach the topic. Some authors consider the angels through stories of human experience; others, through a comparative study of world religions; still others, through the depiction of angels in art and culture. In this book I've tried to draw mostly from the Bible—the inspired Word of God—and also from the saints' reflections on the Scriptures, especially those earliest saints we call the Fathers of the Church. I'll draw practical conclusions whenever possible.

And please visit the Back of the Book, where you'll find prayers, poems and hymns that can deepen your relationship with the angels and help you enter into their heavenly worship and receive their guidance.

Chapter One

What Is an Angel?

. . . .

What *is an angel? It's a simple question, and we already know the* answer. An angel is one of those chubby babies with stubby wings that we remember from Raphael's painting.

But a moment's thought convinces us that that can't be right. After all, what's the first thing angels said when they appeared to people in the Bible? "Don't be afraid!" The appearance of an angel was frightening, even when they came to announce good news. The gut reaction was to fall on the ground.

What *Angel* Means

When we talk about angels, we usually mean any kind of spirit in Scripture. The word *angel* comes from a common Greek word, *angelos*, which means "messenger." We can find it at the heart of words like *"evangelist"* and *"evangelical,"* where it means "news." *Ev-angel* is "good news," the gospel.

So *angel* isn't really so much a name as a job description. "'Angel' is the name of the office, not of the nature," says Saint Augustine, "for what is called an 'angel' in Greek is called a 'messenger' in our language. 'Messenger,' therefore, is the name of the action."[1]

Angels, then, are spirits who bring messages from heaven to earth. We also use the word *angel* to describe all pure spirits—those who worship at the throne of almighty God, those who turn the gears of the cosmos and those who do battle with evil spirits. But the Bible uses a wealth of terms for these creatures: seraphim, cherubim, choirs, thrones, dominions, principalities, powers, sons of God, ministers, servants, hosts, watchers and holy ones.

Think of it this way: When we look up in the sky, we say we see clouds. But a meteorologist sees cumulus, cirrus, nimbus, stratus, cumulonimbus and dozens of other distinct types of clouds. We're not wrong to call them all "clouds," but the meteorologist's distinctions are important when we want to talk about what the clouds are doing—whether they're pleasant and useful rain clouds or whether they plan on knocking down our house.

In the same way we can call any pure spirits "angels," but we have more precise names when we want to make more precise distinctions.

Not all heavenly spirits are messengers, strictly speaking. But heavenly messengers are probably the pure spirits we humans have consciously encountered more than any others. It's the messengers who must make their message known—and often their presence as well. The angel Gabriel not only conversed with Zechariah; he identified himself by name (see Luke 1:19). Raphael did the same for young Tobias (Tobit 12:15).

The Hebrew equivalent of *angelos* is *malach*, the root of the name *Malachi*, the last of the Old Testament prophets. In Hebrew, too, there is a certain ambiguity, and ancient sources disagree about whether the biblical Malachi was a heavenly messenger or an earthly prophet.

The early Christians even referred to Christ as an "angel" from heaven. Writing around AD 150, Justin Martyr sometimes applied the term to Christ. He was especially fond of the prophet Isaiah's promise (in the Septuagint Greek Old Testament) that the Messiah's name would be "Angel of Great Counsel" (Isaiah 9:6).[2]

And it's true, in a sense, to say that Jesus is an "angel" because he is indeed a messenger from heaven. He often spoke of himself in those terms (see, for example, John 17:7–8).

Yet Justin wasn't saying that Jesus is an angel as Michael and Gabriel and Raphael are angels. He made the distinction abundantly clear: Jesus "is called God, and He is and shall be God."[3] The other angels are pure spirits, and in that sense they are *like* God; and they are messengers, and in that sense they are *like* Jesus. But they are creatures, and Christ is their creator.

In Jesus the medium is the message. The messenger is himself the infinite entirety of the message. That's why Christians stopped using the term *angel* to refer to Christ. There was too much potential for confusion.

In the broader sense the evangelists were "angels" because they were messengers of the Good News. And we too are called to be angels because we are called to be apostles—that is, we are sent forth to proclaim a message, glad tidings, Good News, the gospel (see Matthew 28:19–20).

Normally, however, when we talk about "angels," we mean *purely spiritual beings* created by God.

Picturing Angels

Belief in angels is an important part of Christianity, Judaism and Islam. But many other world religions teach of the existence of superhuman spiritual powers, which we might see as angels or at least angellike beings. Even secular philosophers have reasoned their way to the existence of angels. Mortimer Adler wrote a book about the angels, and at the time he identified himself as a pagan!

Adler came up with a helpful phrase to describe angels. He called them "minds without bodies." He noted that it's easy for us to imagine bodies without minds. We see them every day: rocks and trees, for example. They are matter without spirit. It's a little bit harder, though, for us to think about spirit apart from matter.

Yet we do. At every Sunday worship we recite the Nicene Creed, professing our firm belief "in God the Father almighty, creator of heaven and earth, of all things seen and unseen." When we do so we are simply echoing the very first line of the first book of the Bible: "In the beginning God created the heavens and the earth" (Genesis 1:1). When Genesis says, "the heavens and the earth," it is not limiting creation to our little planet and its peculiar atmosphere. It means all of creation, spiritual and material. When God created "the heavens," he was creating not a material place but a spiritual realm. "The heavens" are the "things unseen"—the creatures we commonly know as angels, no matter the nature of their business: watching or worshiping, guarding or messaging.

Still, the idea of "minds without bodies" can be taxing on our minds, which are so dependent on our bodily senses. We are by nature empiricists. Seeing is believing, we say, and, what you *see* is what you get. So we imagine the angels—which can be a help but also can be a hindrance, because they are not cuddly cupids.

Why do we picture them this way? Why do we need to picture them at all?

The Old Testament gives us several images of angels. Often they resemble ordinary humans, as did the angels who visited Lot in Sodom (see Genesis 19). But just as often spiritual beings are something terrifying, as Daniel experienced:

> I lifted up my eyes and looked, and behold, a man clothed in linen, whose loins were belted with gold of Uphaz. His body was like beryl, his face like the appearance of lightning, his eyes like flaming torches, his arms and legs like the gleam of burnished bronze, and the sound of his words like the noise of a multitude. And I, Daniel, alone saw the vision, for the men who were with me did not see the vision, but a great trembling fell upon them, and they fled to hide themselves. So I was left alone and saw this great vision, and no strength was left in me; my radiant appearance was fearfully changed, and I retained no strength. Then I heard the sound of his words; and when I heard the sound of his words, I fell on my face in a deep sleep with my face to the ground.
>
> And behold, a hand touched me and set me trembling on my hands and knees. And he said to me, "O Daniel, man greatly beloved, give heed to the words that I speak to you, and stand upright, for now I have been sent to you." While he was speaking this word to me, I stood up trembling. Then he said to me, "Fear not, Daniel." (Daniel 10:5–12)

From Daniel's description we can see why "Fear not" is often the first thing an angel says. The prophet Ezekiel saw even more fearsome visions:

And from the midst of it came the likeness of four living creatures. And this was their appearance: they had the form of men, but each had four faces, and each of them had four wings. Their legs were straight, and the soles of their feet were like the sole of a calf's foot; and they sparkled like burnished bronze. Under their wings on their four sides they had human hands. And the four had their faces and their wings thus: their wings touched one another; they went every one straight forward, without turning as they went. As for the likeness of their faces, each had the face of a man in front; the four had the face of a lion on the right side, the four had the face of an ox on the left side, and the four had the face of an eagle at the back. Such were their faces. And their wings were spread out above; each creature had two wings, each of which touched the wing of another, while two covered their bodies. And each went straight forward; wherever the spirit would go, they went, without turning as they went. In the midst of the living creatures there was something that looked like burning coals of fire, like torches moving back and forth among the living creatures; and the fire was bright, and out of the fire went forth lightning. And the living creatures darted back and forth, like a flash of lightning. (Ezekiel 1:5–14)

This description is heavily allegorical, but for our purpose the main point is this: The heavenly spirits aren't cuddly. Daniel's reaction to one was to fall flat on his face. And if you saw one of Ezekiel's "living creatures," you'd almost certainly run as fast as you could in the opposite direction.

So why the smiling babies with stubby wings?

Living With Angels

Maybe the cuddly cupids and the chaste Victorian beauties aren't so ridiculous after all. It's true that the cherubim in the Bible are fearsome creatures. But it's also true that the coming of Christ completely changed our relationship with the angels, as we'll see later. The members of Christ's Church now join with the angels in worshiping God. So we can imagine the angels in ways that inspire love rather than fear. If that means we make them look like cute little toddlers with inadequate wings, then perhaps that's just as accurate a representation of what angels mean to a Christian as Daniel's "eyes like flaming torches" was of what angels meant to him.

Are angels people too?

Actually, that's not quite right. We tend to think of *persons* and *people* as equivalent terms, but they're not. Angels are persons, but they are not people. To borrow from the singers David Lee Roth and Louis Prima, the angels "ain't got no body."

In the animal kingdom there is only one type of spiritual being: man. But our spirits are united to our bodies. That gives us a unique position in the universe.

> Brute creatures both are and live and feel, yet do not understand. Angels both are and live and feel, and by understanding they exercise discernment. Man, then, in that he has it in common with stones to be, with trees to live, with animals to feel, with angels to discern, is rightly represented by the title of the "universe," in whom after some sort the "universe" itself is contained.[4]

The spiritual beings in the "heavens" are pure spirit. They are bodiless, which means they are not limited by the bodily things that limit us. They can appear to be embodied, like humans, but that is only an appearance, assumed for our sake—an accommodation to our weakness.

Although angels are nonmaterial, they can affect matter. The devil disputed with Michael over the *body* of Moses (see Jude 9); they must have been at odds over its movement or disposal. When Daniel was in the lions' den, it was an angel who "shut the lions' mouths" (Daniel 6:22), just as an angel had kept the three youths cool in the white-hot fiery furnace (Daniel 3:26–27).

Angels are persons. They can think, love and make choices. Like us, they have intellect and free will—though their intellects make our own seem hardly worthy of the title; and their will is perfectly aligned with God's (at least in the case of the good angels), whereas our wills tend to veer and waver.

The fixity of the angelic will is the reason why we pray, in the Lord's Prayer, that God's "will be done on earth as it is *in heaven*." Here again, *heaven* means the realm of the spirits, not the expanse of the galaxies. We're praying not that we might be more predictable, like planets and asteroids, but that we might be as morally sure and true as the angels are.

THE NATURAL HISTORY OF ANGELS

So what do we really know about angels?

We can't study them in the same way we study jaguars or amoebas. They don't trip camera traps, and they don't show up under microscopes. What we know about them comes from what the Bible and Tradition tell us and from what reason can deduce.

Angels are pure spirits. They have a beginning but not an end. Angels were created by God, and they were created immortal. They have no gender. They do not reproduce.

We don't know the population of angels. But knowing that everybody who has ever lived has had a guardian angel—and assuming that no one's gets recycled—we can bet that there are plenty of them. Remember, guardian angels are just one subset of the pure spirits.

Each angel is unique. In fact, philosophers and theologians say that each angel is a unique species. Animal species are differentiated by bodily features, which angels lack. And so we cannot group two or more of them together as we do human beings, mice and raccoons.

So in fact we know a good bit about the angels. They are like God in being purely spiritual beings, immortal and without bodies. But they are like us in having been created by God and in being limited rather than omnipotent. They are somewhat like God and somewhat like us, yet quite unlike both God and us.

This may sound like an unpromising beginning to our study, but it served very well for one of history's greatest experts on the angels, Saint Gregory the Great. Saint Gregory served as pope from AD 590 to 604, and he wrote extensively about the heavenly hosts. He gathered the teachings of the earlier Church Fathers and organized them in a way that was both systematic and pastoral. Gregory's biographers tell us that he had some dramatic, close encounters with angels as well. We'll be calling upon him quite often as we pursue our own angelic studies in this book.

Saint Gregory drew a wealth of conclusions from those basic principles about angels and sketched a kind of profile for us:

This is how the nature of angels is different from the present condition of our own nature: we are both circumscribed by space, and limited by the blindness of ignorance; but the spirits of angels are indeed bounded by space, yet their knowledge extends far above us beyond comparison; for they expand by external and internal knowing, since they contemplate the very source of knowledge itself.

For of those things that are capable of being known, what is there that they do not know? For they know him, to Whom all things are known. So that their knowledge when compared with ours is vastly extended, yet in comparison with the divine knowledge it is little. In like manner, their very spirits in comparison with our bodies are spirits, but compared with the supreme and incomprehensible Spirit, they are body.

Therefore they are both sent from him, and remain by him too. Being circumscribed, they go forth; but being also entirely present, they never go away. Thus at the same time they always behold the Father's face, and yet they come to us; because they both go forth to us in a spiritual presence, and yet keep themselves in the place from which they had gone out, by virtue of interior contemplation. It may then be said, "The sons of God came to present themselves before the Lord"; inasmuch as they come back there by a return of the spirit, though they never depart from there by any withdrawal of the mind.[5]

Now, there is one other very important way in which the angels are like us: The angels were created with free will. They could accept or reject God, and not all of them made the right choice.

 THE TESTING OF ANGELS

> For long ago you broke your yoke
> and burst your bonds;
> and you said, "I will not serve."
> (Jeremiah 2:20)

. . . . .

E*very being with free will has a choice to make. Will you serve God, or* won't you? This free choice affects everything that follows.

The heavenly spirits always do God's will, and they do it by their own free choice. But not all the spirits are in heaven. What about the others—the "fallen angels"? What happened to them?

It's hard to say, since angels' lives are so much different from ours. Theologians speculate that angels were given that all-important choice at the moment of their creation. As one of Saint John's letters tells us, "the devil has sinned from the beginning" (1 John 3:8). But there is no specific story of the fall of the fallen angels. The event is simply assumed in Scripture. Jesus said to his seventy disciples: "I saw Satan fall like lightning from heaven" (Luke 10:18).

A predominant image of Satan's fall comes from John Milton, whose *Paradise Lost* is almost certainly the most famous English epic. There he wrote:

He trusted to have equaled the Most High,
If He opposed, and, with ambitious aim
Against the throne and monarchy of God,
Raised impious war in Heaven and battle proud
With vain attempt. Him the Almighty Power
Hurled headlong flaming from the ethereal sky,
With hideous ruin and combustion, down
To bottomless perdition, there to dwell
In adamantine chains and penal fire,
Who durst defy the Omnipotent to arms.[1]

We may not have the whole story, but we do know that the angels faced the same choice that humanity faced, and that some of them made the wrong choice. But how is it possible for spiritual beings to go bad? Weren't they created perfect?

Yes, they were—but remember, so were we.

CAN ANGELS CHANGE?

The question of whether angels can change was a tough one for philosophers and theologians. Gregory the Great attacked the thorny problem and reasoned it out thoroughly:

The nature of angels is fixed in contemplation of the Creator, and so it remains unchangeable in its own state. Yet because it is a created being, it admits in itself the variableness of change.

Now to be changed is to go from one thing into another, and to be without stability in one's self. For every single being tends to some other thing by steps, as many in number as it is subject to motions of change. Only the Incomprehensible Nature cannot be moved from its fixed state: it is always the same, and it cannot be changed.

> For if the essence of the angels had been incapable of the motion of change, created well by its Maker, it would never have fallen in the case of reprobate spirits from the tower of its blessed estate. But Almighty God, in a marvelous manner, made the nature of the highest spiritual beings good, yet at the same time capable of change. In this way the ones that refused to remain might meet with ruin; but the ones that continued in their own state of creation might henceforth be established in that state more worthily, to the degree that it was due to their own choice, and become so much the more meritorious in God's sight, as they had stayed the motion of their mutability by the establishing of the will.[2]

So the fall of some of the angels from perfection heightens the honor of the countless legions who remained to serve God faithfully.

But we are left to wonder why some did fall. What would lead them to prefer hell to heaven? The book of Wisdom tells us: "Through the devil's envy death entered the world, / and those who belong to his party experience it" (Wisdom 2:23–24).

It was envy that led Satan to rebel. We often say that Satan's characteristic sin is pride. The two sins are closely related. Satan couldn't bear the thought that there was a Being greater than he was. He meant to rule, not to be ruled. Like the Israelites in the book of Jeremiah, he stared God in the face and said, "I will not serve." In that pride and envy, Satan started a war he couldn't win. "God did not spare the angels when they sinned, but cast them into hell and committed them to pits of deepest darkness to be kept until the judgment" (2 Peter 2:4).

But banishment did not cure Satan's pride. We don't know exactly what Satan thinks—no human can really know exactly what the angels think. But he seems to have decided, in Milton's words,

> Here we may reign secure; and, in my choice,
> To reign is worth ambition, though in Hell;
> Better to reign in Hell than serve in Heaven.[3]

More than that, Satan decided that, if he was going down, he wasn't going down alone. He took a third of the angels with him, according to the symbolic vision of Revelation: "And another sign appeared in heaven; behold, a great red dragon, with seven heads and ten horns, and seven diadems upon his heads. His tail swept down a third of the stars of heaven, and cast them to the earth" (Revelation 12:3–4).

The dragon and his angels went to war against the angels of heaven, led by Saint Michael. It ended with complete defeat for Satan: "And the great dragon was thrown down, that ancient serpent, who is called the Devil and Satan, the deceiver of the whole world—he was thrown down to the earth, and his angels were thrown down with him" (Revelation 12:9).

Revelation leaves us in no doubt about whom we're dealing with. And that reminds us that the next chapter in Satan's story is found way back in Genesis.

DOWN IN THE GARDEN

Now the serpent was more subtle than any other wild creature that the LORD God had made. He said to the woman, "Did God say, 'You shall not eat of any tree of the garden'?" And the woman said to the serpent, "We may eat of the fruit of the trees of the garden; but God said, 'You shall not eat of the fruit of the tree which is in the midst of the garden, neither shall you touch it, lest you die.'" But the serpent said to the woman, "You will not die. For God knows that when you eat of it your eyes will be opened, and you will be like God, knowing good and evil." So when the woman saw that the tree was good for food, and that it was a delight to the eyes, and that the tree was to be desired to make one wise, she took of its fruit and ate; and she also gave some to her husband, and he ate. (Genesis 3:1–6)

Satan couldn't bear to see God's new creatures living in harmony with their Creator. If he was doomed, then he would do his best to spoil things for everybody. As the *Catechism of the Catholic Church* puts it, "Behind the disobedient choice of our first parents lurks a seductive voice, opposed to God, which makes them fall into death out of envy. Scripture and the Church's Tradition see in this being a fallen angel, called 'Satan' or the 'devil'" (CCC, 391).

Satan was successful—for a time. Adam and Eve were expelled from the Garden, and cherubim were set to guard the gates of Eden. Yet fallen though God's human creatures were, they had not fallen quite as far as Satan. Even as God pronounced the inevitable judgment on them, he also promised his people a redeemer:

The LORD God said to the serpent,
"Because you have done this,
   cursed are you above all cattle,
   and above all wild animals;
upon your belly you shall go,
   and dust you shall eat
   all the days of your life.
I will put enmity between you and the woman,

> and between your seed and her seed;
> he shall bruise your head,
> and you shall bruise his heel." (Genesis 3:14–15)

Christians have always seen these verses as the *protoevangelium* or "first gospel," a prediction of the coming of the Christ, the "seed" of a woman, who would crush the head of Satan. And in that promise of redemption is the difference between the fall of angels and the fall of humanity. The intractable will of Satan is in a constant state of defiance; we, on the other hand, have the possibility of redemption through Jesus Christ.

Saint Gregory the Great put it very well:

> Now he had made two creations to contemplate himself, the angelic and the human. But pride struck both, and dashed them from the erect station of native uprightness. But one had the clothing of the flesh, the other bore no infirmity derived from the flesh. For an angelical being is spirit alone, but man is both spirit and flesh. Therefore when the Creator took compassion to work redemption, it was appropriate that he should bring back to himself that creature, which, in the commission of sin, plainly had something of infirmity; and it was also appropriate that the apostate Angel should be driven down to a farther depth, in proportion as he, when he fell from resoluteness in standing fast, carried about him no infirmity of the flesh.[4]

The really tragic part of the story of Satan is that God loves him still—him and all his followers. "It is the *irrevocable* character of their choice, and not a defect in the infinite divine mercy, that makes the angels' sin unforgivable" (CCC, 393). God has never stopped loving them, but they have cut themselves off from God's love by their own pride and envy.

Opposed but Not Opposite

So we know that there are bad angels, and we know that they have set themselves in opposition to God. Does that mean that Satan is somehow the "opposite of God"—an all-powerful evil that balances God's all-powerful goodness?

No. It's very important for us to recognize that Satan is *not* God's opposite. God is all-powerful; Satan is not. God is all-knowing; Satan knows a lot, but he can't know all the things God knows. He doesn't know the details of God's plan of salvation. And he can't do anything to stop the fulfillment of God's plan.

The Council of Braga (in AD 561) declared that the devil was created by God and was created good, and that he cannot create anything himself. This is important to remember, because the council was addressing "dualist" heresies of the time. Dualism is the idea that there are two equal forces in the universe, one good and one evil. It seems to be just as attractive today as it was back then. Think of George Lucas's "force" in *Star Wars,* with its balanced light and dark sides.

The devil is not an eternal principle of evil as God is the eternal principle of goodness. The devil is not eternal: He is finite; he had a beginning. God created the devil and all the rebel angels, and he created them very good. It was their own will that made them fall, but they are still God's creations.

Chapter Three

 ANGELS IN THE OLD TESTAMENT

. . . .

W*hen God's people set to writing their story, they told the tale with* great economy, mentioning only the details that truly mattered. They were doing more than just keeping good records: They were telling us how to understand our own life stories.

They could not conceive of a human drama that did not involve angel players. The drama of creation, the drama of the patriarchs, the drama of the Exodus, the drama of the kingdom —these turned on angelic activity. "Nearly every page of Scripture testifies to the existence of angels and archangels," said Saint Gregory the Great.[1]

These angels had many roles in the Old Testament, and perhaps the best way to look at them is to look at what they did. If we were to examine all the Old Testament's angel interventions, this book would need to be much longer than my publisher would allow. But let's take a fresh look at some representative stories, so that we truly read what the authors wrote, and we restore the angels to their rightful place.

When we read the Bible with our eyes open for angels, we notice that they are not ornaments on the picture frame or convenient plot devices. They're in the foreground and the background. They play starring roles, center stage.

MESSENGERS OF GOD

Angels, the messengers of God, bring the Word of God to women and men in the Bible. This is their most familiar role and the one from which they get their name.

Sometimes an angel came to announce an important birth. Such was the message that three visitors—perhaps angels, perhaps the Lord himself—brought Abraham (see Genesis 18:1–15). And when Israel had been oppressed by the Philistines for a long time, an angel came to the wife of Manoah to announce: "Behold, you are barren and have no children; but you shall conceive and bear a son. Therefore beware, and drink no wine or strong drink, and eat nothing unclean, for behold, you shall conceive and bear a son. No razor shall come upon his head, for the boy shall be a Nazirite to God from birth; and he shall begin to deliver Israel from the hand of the Philistines" (Judges 13:3–5).

This son of Manoah was Samson, the mighty hero who would save Israel from the Philistines.

Sometimes the news an angel brought wasn't quite so good. When Balaam the seer was on his way to curse the Israelites (he was doing a sort of consulting job for Balak, the king of Moab), "God's anger was kindled" (Numbers 22:22). What follows is a comical talking-animal story that shows what a fearsome thing meeting an angel could be:

The angel of the Lord took his stand in the way as his adversary.

…. And [Balaam's] donkey saw the angel of the LORD standing in the road, with a drawn sword in his hand; and the donkey turned aside out of the road, and went into the field; and

Balaam struck the donkey, to turn her into the road. Then the angel of the LORD stood in a narrow path between the vineyards, with a wall on either side. And when the donkey saw the angel of the LORD, she pushed against the wall, and pressed Balaam's foot against the wall; so he struck her again. Then the angel of the LORD went ahead, and stood in a narrow place, where there was no way to turn either to the right or to the left. When the donkey saw the angel of the LORD, she lay down under Balaam; and Balaam's anger was kindled, and he struck the donkey with his staff. Then the LORD opened the mouth of the donkey, and she said to Balaam, "What have I done to you, that you have struck me these three times?" And Balaam said to the donkey, "Because you have made sport of me. I wish I had a sword in my hand, for then I would kill you." And the donkey said to Balaam, "Am I not your donkey, upon which you have ridden all your life long to this day? Was I ever accustomed to do so to you?" And he said, "No."

Then the LORD opened the eyes of Balaam, and he saw the angel of the LORD standing in the way, with his drawn sword in his hand; and he bowed his head, and fell on his face. And the angel of the LORD said to him, "Why have you struck your donkey these three times? Behold, I have come forth to withstand you, because your way is perverse before me; and the donkey saw me, and turned aside before me these three times. If she had not turned aside from me, surely just now I would have slain you and let her live." Then Balaam said to the angel of the LORD, "I have sinned, for I did not know that you stood in the road against me. Now therefore, if it is evil in your sight, I will go back again." And the angel of the LORD said to Balaam, "Go with the men; but only the word which I bid you, that shall you speak." So Balaam went on with the princes of Balak. (Numbers 22:22, 23–35)

Angels even brought messages to the prophets.

HELPERS IN TIMES OF NEED

Angels were often sent to give help to people who desperately needed it. Usually these were people who had a job to do: God sent his angel not only to help them but also to encourage them and to remind them to get on with it.

Hagar, Abraham's second wife, is a good example. She had two angelic visits, each one at a time when she might otherwise have died alone in the desert. The first time is actually the first occurrence of the word *angel* in the Bible.

Hagar's relationship with Sarai (later Sarah), Abraham's first wife, had become so bad that she ran out into the desert to escape:

> The angel of the LORD found her by a spring of water in the wilderness, the spring on the way to Shur. And he said, "Hagar, maid of Sarai, where have you come from and where are you going?" She said, "I am fleeing from my mistress Sarai." The angel of the LORD said to her, "Return to your mistress, and submit to her." The angel of the LORD also said to her, "I will so greatly multiply your descendants that they cannot be numbered for multitude." And the angel of the LORD said to her, "Behold, you are with child, and shall bear a son; you shall call his name Ishmael; because the LORD has given heed to your affliction. He shall be a wild donkey of a man, his hand against every man and every man's hand against him; and he shall dwell over against all his kinsmen." (Genesis 16:7–12)

Here the angel saved Hagar from self-destruction by revealing that she had an important part to play in the divine plan.

But Sarai continued to make trouble for Hagar. Finally forced out of the family and into the desert by Sarai's jealousy, Hagar and her son Ishmael were on the verge of dying.

> She cast the child under one of the bushes. Then she went, and sat down over against him a good way off, about the distance of a bowshot; for she said, "Let me not look upon the death of the child." And as she sat over against him, the child lifted up his voice and wept. And God heard the voice of the lad; and the angel of God called to Hagar from heaven, and said to her, "What troubles you, Hagar? Fear not; for God has heard the voice of the lad where he is. Arise, lift up the lad, and hold him fast with your hand; for I will make him a great nation." Then God opened her eyes, and she saw a well of water; and she went, and filled the skin with water, and gave the lad a drink. (Genesis 21:15–19)

Once again the angel saved Hagar from dying in the desert, and once again he encouraged her by reminding her that she had a job to do.

When God's people undertook a perilous journey for his sake, God sometimes sent his angel to guide the way. When Abraham sent his servant to find a wife for Isaac, Abraham confidently promised him, "The LORD, before whom I walk, will send his angel with you and prosper your way" (Genesis 24:40). An angel guided the people of Israel through the wilderness and into the land of Canaan (see Exodus 14:19; 23:23).

Perhaps the most beloved story of an angel guide is the story of Tobias, who looked for a man to go with him on a perilous journey: "And he found Raphael, who was an angel, but Tobias did not know it" (Tobit 5:4). This story is such a good one, I've included more details about it in chapter ten, which is all about Saint Raphael.

JACOB AND THE ANGELS

The patriarch Jacob had at least three notable angelic visions in his travels. The first one has given the name "Jacob's ladder" to things as diverse as delicate wildflowers and mad scientists' lab equipment:

> Jacob...came to a certain place, and stayed there that night, because the sun had set. Taking one of the stones of the place, he put it under his head and lay down in that place to sleep. And he dreamed that there was a ladder set up on the earth, and the top of it reached to heaven; and behold, the angels of God were ascending and descending on it! And behold, the LORD stood above it and said, "I am the LORD, the God of Abraham your father and the God of Isaac; the land on which you lie I will give to you and to your descendants; and your descendants shall be like the dust of the earth, and you shall spread abroad to the west and to the east and to the north and to the south; and by you and your descendants shall all the families of the earth bless themselves. Behold, I am with you and will keep you wherever you go, and will bring you back to this land; for I will not leave you until I have done that of which I have spoken to you." Then Jacob awoke from his sleep and said, "Surely the LORD is in this place; and I did not know it." And he was afraid, and said, "How awesome is this place! This is none other than the house of God, and this is the gate of heaven." (Genesis 28:10–17)

When Jacob was preparing to meet Esau, the older brother he had tricked out of his inheritance years before, he had a vision of a heavenly host: "Jacob went on his way and the angels of God met him; and when Jacob saw them he said, 'This is God's army!' So he called the name of that place Mahanaim" (Genesis 32:1–2).

Nothing more is said of this vision. It is as though there was nothing out of the ordinary about walking down the road and meeting an army of angels along the way. And for Jacob, that may well have been true.

He spent that night in the wilderness.

> And Jacob was left alone; and a man wrestled with him until the breaking of the day. When the man saw that he did not prevail against Jacob, he touched the hollow of his thigh; and Jacob's thigh was put out of joint as he wrestled with him. Then he said, "Let me go, for the day is breaking." But Jacob said, "I will not let you go, unless you bless me." And he said to him, "What is your name?" And he said, "Jacob." Then he said, "Your name shall no more be called Jacob, but Israel, for you have striven with God and with men, and have prevailed." Then Jacob asked him, "Tell me, I pray, your name." But he said, "Why is it that you ask my name?" And there he blessed him. So Jacob called the name of the place Peniel, saying, "For I have seen God face to face, and yet my life is preserved." (Genesis 32:24–30)

We usually remember this story as "Jacob wrestling with the angel," and many artists have painted it that way. But not everyone agrees on exactly who was wrestling with Jacob. Many early Christian thinkers were of the opinion that it was an angel; but

Origen, the great third-century biblical scholar, thought it was a demon; and others thought it was Christ.

Jacob's name for the place seems to suggest that it was God: "For I have seen God face to face, and yet my life is preserved." Just as in the story of Abraham and his three visitors, it is not always easy to make the distinction between God and his angels in Old Testament stories.

When we come to the New Testament, we find angels doing the same jobs they did in the Old Testament. But we also find that *our* relationship with them is completely different from that of the Old Testament heroes.

Chapter Four

Angels in the New Testament

· · · · · ·

Angels are everywhere in the New Testament too, just as they are in the Old Testament. But there's a very important difference: In the Old Testament the angels are, in a manner of speaking, superiors; now they are our brothers.

The difference is Christ. Paul explains that the angels were guardians in the Old Testament: The Israelites were like children, who couldn't be allowed to take care of themselves. "Why then the law? It was added because of transgressions, till the offspring should come to whom the promise had been made; and it was ordained by angels through an intermediary" (Galatians 3:19).

Paul elaborates in the next chapter:

> I mean that the heir, as long as he is a child, is no better than a slave, though he is the owner of all the estate; but he is under guardians and trustees until the date set by the father. So with us; when we were children, we were slaves to the elemental spirits of the universe. But when the time had fully come, God sent forth his Son, born of woman, born under the law, to redeem those who were under the law, so that we might receive adoption as sons. (Galatians 4:1–5)

The Gospel writers are especially careful to show how the angels serve Jesus Christ in the same way they serve God. From even before his birth, Jesus was surrounded, protected and glorified by angels.

The Annunciation may be the best-known angel appearance in Scripture:

> In the sixth month the angel Gabriel was sent from God to a city of Galilee named Nazareth, to a virgin betrothed to a man whose name was Joseph, of the house of David; and the virgin's name was Mary. And he came to her and said, "Hail, full of grace, the Lord is with you!" But she was greatly troubled at the saying, and considered in her mind what sort of greeting this might be. And the angel said to her, "Do not be afraid, Mary, for you have found favor with God. And behold, you will conceive in your womb and bear a son, and you shall call his name Jesus.
> He will be great, and will be called the Son of
>   the Most High;
> and the Lord God will give to him the throne of
>   his father David,
> and he will reign over the house of Jacob for
>   ever;
> and of his kingdom there will be no end." (Luke 1:26–33)

This appearance of Gabriel is a lot like the angelic announcements in the Old Testament. It might remind us especially of the announcement of Samson's birth: An angel comes to a woman to announce that she will bear a son who will save Israel. But there's a noticeable difference in tone.

When Gabriel—who's not just an angel, remember, but an archangel—approached Mary, he started right off showing respect to her. She, the human being of flesh and blood, was greeted by an archangel as if she were in some way his superior.

An angel also appeared to Joseph to explain the situation:

> When his mother Mary had been betrothed to Joseph, before they came together she was found to be with child of the Holy Spirit; and her husband Joseph, being a just man and unwilling to put her to shame, resolved to send her away quietly. But as he considered this, behold, an angel of the Lord appeared to him in a dream, saying, "Joseph, son of David, do not fear to take Mary your wife, for that which is conceived in her is of the Holy Spirit; she will bear a son, and you shall call his name Jesus, for he will save his people from their sins."
> (Matthew 1:18–21)

At the birth of Jesus, angels sang hymns of praise to God: "Glory to God in the highest, / and on earth peace among men with whom he / is pleased!" (Luke 2:14). And after his birth they continue to surround and protect him. When Herod plotted to kill the helpless infant, an angel appeared to Joseph, warning him to flee to Egypt. An angel appeared to Joseph again when the danger was over, telling him to go back to Palestine.

Angels also appeared to announce the Resurrection. "Two men...in dazzling apparel" said to the women who came to the tomb, "Why do you seek the living among the dead? He is not here, but has risen" (Luke 24:4–5).

Angels trumpeted the beginning and the end of Christ's career. And that shouldn't surprise us. Angels are, after all, messengers by trade, bringing the Word of God. And Jesus Christ is the Word incarnate. Angels are messengers, and Jesus is their message.

CHRIST, LORD OF HOSTS

Throughout the Gospels we're reminded of the association of Jesus with angels. Often Jesus himself made that association, especially when he spoke of the Last Judgment: "Just as the weeds are gathered and burned with fire, so will it be at the close of the age. The Son of man will send his angels, and they will gather out of his kingdom all causes of sin and all evildoers, and throw them into the furnace of fire, where there will be weeping and gnashing of teeth" (Matthew 13:40–42).

When Christ returns at the end of the age, he will come in the company of angels. "For whoever is ashamed of me and of my words in this adulterous and sinful generation, of him will the Son of man also be ashamed, when he comes in the glory of his Father with the holy angels" (Mark 8:38).

This constant association with angels led Jesus' hearers to one conclusion: Incredible as it might sound, Jesus was proclaiming that he was somehow divine. Jesus promised the apostle Nathanael that he would see marvels: "Truly, truly, I say to you, you will see heaven opened, and the angels of God ascending and descending upon the Son of man" (John 1:51).

Angels didn't just surround Jesus; they served him too. Just after his temptation in the desert, Matthew tells us, "the devil left him, and behold, angels came and ministered to him" (Matthew 4:11).

And at the moment of his betrayal, Jesus reminded his disciples that he could call on the angels to defend him: "Put your sword back into its place; for all who take the sword will perish by the sword. Do you think that I cannot appeal to my Father, and he will at once send me more than twelve legions of angels? But how then should the Scriptures be fulfilled, that it must be so?" (Matthew 26:52–54).

The shocking truth is that angels in the New Testament treated Christ the same way they treated God in the Old Testament. Even though he was, for a time, a little less than the angels, they served him, praised him, sang hymns to his glory and attended him. Christ is nothing less than the One whom the Old Testament proclaims as "the LORD of hosts"—the commander of the hosts of angels (see 2 Samuel 7:26; Psalm 24:10; Isaiah 1:9).

The Letter to the Hebrews dwells at some length on the superiority of Christ to the angels:

> He reflects the glory of God and bears the very stamp of his nature, upholding the universe by his word of power. When he had made purification for sins, he sat down at the right hand of the Majesty on high, having become as much superior to angels as the name he has obtained is more excellent than theirs.
>
> For to what angel did God ever say,
>> "You are my Son,
>>
>> today I have begotten you"?
>
> Or again,
>> "I will be to him a father,
>>
>> and he shall be to me a son"?
>
> And again, when he brings the first-born into the world, he says,
>> "Let all God's angels worship him." (Hebrews 1:3–6)

The First Letter of Peter also puts Christ in the place of God, with the angels subject to him: "Jesus Christ...has gone into heaven and is at the right hand of God, with angels, authorities, and powers subject to him" (1 Peter 3:21–22).

All these things show that Christ is the Son of God, who bears the same relationship to the angels that God the Father does.

WE ARE TO JUDGE ANGELS

All this has been true since the beginning of time: God the Son has always been God. But the Incarnation changed our own relationship with the angels. Saint Gregory the Great explains:

> Before the birth of our redeemer, we had lost the friendship of the angels. Original sin and our daily sins had kept us away from their bright purity.... But ever since the moment we acknowledged our king, the angels have recognized us as their fellow citizens.
>
> And seeing that the king of heaven wished to take on our earthly flesh, the angels no longer shun our misery. They do not dare consider as inferior to their own this nature which they adore in the person of the king of heaven; there it is, raised up above them; they have now no difficulty in regarding man as companion.[1]

We are companions to the angels! As incredible as it seems, the Incarnation has lifted us up to a kind of equality with the powerful spirits of heaven. When people of the Old Testament fell on their faces in front of angels, the angels were often content to leave them there. But when Saint John bowed down before an angel, the angel told him, "You must not do that! I am a fellow servant with you and your brethren who hold the testimony of Jesus. Worship God" (Revelation 19:10).

This should be amazing enough: angels calling themselves "fellow servants" with us puny humans. But in some ways we have *even more* than equality with the angels.

In Christ our humanity is assumed to God. "If we endure, we shall also reign with him" (2 Timothy 2:12), and so we render judgment with him. And whom do we judge? "Do you not know that we are to judge angels?" Saint Paul asked rhetorically (1 Corinthians 6:3). It's an amazing idea: We, mere creatures of flesh and blood, will judge powerful spirits!

And if that weren't startling enough, Saint Peter talks about "the things which have now been announced to you by those who preached the good news to you through the Holy Spirit sent from heaven, things into which angels long to look" (1 Peter 1:12). It seems that we know things that weren't revealed to the angels!

Reflecting on such Scriptures, Saint Ignatius of Loyola marveled that God "has placed under our ministry, not only all that is under heaven but even the whole of His sublime court, not excepting even any of the heavenly hierarchy."[2] The angels, who were once our caretakers, are now, in a very real sense, subject to our ministry!

This is what it means for us to share in the reign of Christ. The Son of God became our brother, so that we also might be daughters and sons of God.

This authority is over the fallen angels also. When Christ pronounces judgment on the evil angels who have tormented us, we make that judgment with him. Our brotherhood with Christ gives us a share in his power over the evil angels—more about this in chapter eleven.

THE ANGELS JUDGE TOO

Yet lest we go back to picturing the angels as cuddly toddlers with stubby wings, we should remember that, to sinners, the angels remain fearsome instruments of judgment. Jesus won't let us forget that. Explaining his parable of the weeds sown with the wheat, he told his disciples:

> Just as the weeds are gathered and burned with fire, so will it be at the close of the age. The Son of man will send his angels, and they will gather out of his kingdom all causes of sin and all evildoers, and throw them into the furnace of fire, where there will be weeping and gnashing of teeth. (Matthew 13:40–42)

Jesus repeated that message in another parable:

> Again, the kingdom of heaven is like a net which was thrown into the sea and gathered fish of every kind; when it was full, men drew it ashore and sat down and sorted the good into vessels but threw away the bad. So it will be at the close of the age. The angels will come out and separate the evil from the righteous, and throw them into the furnace of fire, where there will be weeping and gnashing of teeth. (Matthew 13:47–50)

Such words perhaps strike fear in our hearts. But they're really words of great comfort. For we won't be lost in the morass of sin and evil that the world often seems to be. If we endure with Christ, we'll reign with Christ. And at the end of the age, the angels will come to take us away from the encircling gloom. They'll know who we are—our Brother, Jesus Christ, will already have pointed us out to them.

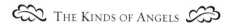

THE KINDS OF ANGELS

. . . .

Scripture speaks of many kinds of pure spirits, each kind apparently distinct from the others. We read a lot about angels, but we also hear of *seraphim* (Isaiah 6:2), *cherubim* (Ezekiel 10:1–3), *archangels* (1 Thessalonians 4:16), *ministering spirits* (Hebrews 1:14), *holy ones* (Psalm 89:5,7), the *host of the heavens* (Psalm 33:6) and *sons of God* (Job 1:6). Saint Paul mentions *angels, thrones, dominions, principalities, powers, authorities, world rulers* and *spiritual hosts*—a whole spiritual ecology (Colossians 1:16; Romans 8:38; Ephesians 6:12).

There are certainly differences in angels. Yet Scripture nowhere says what those differences might be, or how one kind of angel might rank in relation to the others. Saint Paul speaks of them as if they exist according to a certain order. But he does not elaborate.

This has roused the curiosity of some of the great souls of the Christian tradition. Though the Bible gives no explicit ranking of the angelic hierarchy, many of the Bible's greatest interpreters believed such a ranking was implicit in the sacred page, and they pored over every angel reference for clues. Surely too, they enjoyed angelic guidance. Nevertheless, the Church has never made any dogmatic pronouncements on the ranking of angels.

HIERARCHIES OF ANGELS

The classic commentator on the angelic hierarchies was a Christian, probably of the sixth century, who wrote under the name "Dionysius the Areopagite" (see Acts 17:34). In English translations he is often called Saint Denis. It was he who coined the word *hierarchia* (literally, "sacred order") to describe the ranking of angels; and it was he who laid the foundations for the later speculations of Saint Gregory, Saint Thomas, Saint Bonaventure and others.

One of these masters of angelology, Saint Gregory the Great, laid out for us the reasoning on hierarchies:

> We know on the authority of Scripture that there are nine orders of angels, viz., Angels, Archangels, Virtues, Powers, Principalities, Dominations, Thrones, Cherubim and Seraphim. That there are Angels and Archangels nearly every page of the Bible tells us, and the books of the Prophets talk of Cherubim, and Seraphim.... St. Paul, too, writing to the Ephesians enumerates four orders when he says: "above all Principality, and Power, and Virtue, and Domination"; and again, writing to the Colossians he says: "whether Thrones, or Dominations, or Principalities, or Powers." If we now join these two lists together we have five Orders, and adding Angels and Archangels, Cherubim and Seraphim, we find nine Orders of Angels.[1]

Centuries later Saint Thomas Aquinas, the great master of system, would refine the list, dividing it into three hierarchies of three orders each:

I. First hierarchy:
  Seraphim
  Cherubim
  Thrones

II. Second Hierarchy:
  Dominations (or *Dominions*)
  Virtues (or *Authorities*)
  Powers

III. Third Hierarchy:
  Principalities
  Archangels
  Angels

Saint Thomas divides the angels based on how near they are to God, the closest being the seraphim. This is careful speculation based on an exceptionally careful reading of Scripture; it is not official Church doctrine. Nevertheless, if we read the Bible with any care, it's impossible to escape the conclusion that there must be *some* hierarchy of spiritual beings.

Saint Gregory presented a stunning panorama, covering the heavens and the earth:

> Likewise man is over the beasts, the Angels over man, and the Archangels are set over the Angels.
>
> Now that man has sovereignty over the beasts, we both perceive by the common use, and are instructed by the words of the Psalmist, who says, "Thou hast put all things under his feet; all sheep and oxen, yea, and the beasts of the field" (Ps. 8: 6–7).

And that the Angels are placed over man is testified by the Prophet, in these words, "But the prince of the kingdom of Persia withstood me" (Daniel 10:13).

And that the Angels are under the governance of authority in superior Angels, the Prophet Zechariah declares: *And, behold, the angel that talked with me went forth, and another angel went out to meet him, and he said unto him, Run, speak to this young man, saying, Jerusalem shall be inhabited as towns without walls* (Zechariah 2:3–4). For in the actual ministration of the holy spirits, if the superior Powers did not direct the inferior, one angel would never have learnt from the lips of another what he should say to a man.

Therefore, since the Creator of the universe holds all things by himself alone, and yet for the purpose of constituting the defined order characterizing a universe of beauty, he rules one part by the governance of another; we shall not improperly understand the kings to be the angelic spirits, who the more devotedly they serve the Maker of all beings, have things subject to their rule the more.[2]

AUTHORIZED TO SERVE

As citizens of a modern democracy, we tend to bristle at talk of hierarchy. The question arises unbidden: Why aren't all the angels equal? And then, perhaps, further questions come up. Why should there be angels at all? If God is all-powerful, why doesn't he just accomplish his works by executive order—by divine decree? These are the questions behind many of the most common objections to Catholic devotion and study of the angels.

Well, of course God can do anything directly, without any intermediaries. He is perfectly free and not bound to do anything the way he's done it. He did not even need to create anything—nevermind arrange it all in a hierarchy. But he did; and since he is all-wise, he did it in the way that is most fitting.

God created a universe full of beings that are *interdependent*—beings who need one another, who might serve one another, who might love one another, all to reflect his life, all to his greater glory. The earth is full of God's mediators, and so are the heavens. The Bible tells us so. Our Father wanted to do it this way, and we can be glad for that.

In our imperfect world *authority* usually means "power," and power usually means the ability to get what you want. People grasp at power more greedily than they grasp at wealth, and once they grasp it they go to any extreme to hold on to it.

In the heavenly arrangement authority is always *the power to do good,* and more authority is the power to do more good. So the hierarchy is not for the benefit of the people with the most power but rather to lift up the people with the least power. Saint Denis explains:

> The purpose of hierarchy is to enable beings, as much as possible, to be like God and have union with Him. The hierarchy has God as its Leader in all knowledge and activity. A hierarchy looks unflinchingly at His most divine beauty.
>
> A hierarchy, as much as possible, perfects its own followers to be divine images, luminous and flawless reflections, receiving the primal light in its supremely divine ray. When the followers are devoutly filled, the hierarchy ensures that they spread this radiance unsparingly to those lower beings, according to God's will.[3]

A hierarchy is literally a sacred order. It is an order of love, and so it is an order of service. Christ is at the head of all hierarchy, not merely because he has power but because he serves all. Christ himself said, "Whoever would be great among you must be your servant, and whoever would be first among you must be your slave; even as the Son of man came not to be served but to serve, and to give his life as a ransom for many" (Matthew 20:26–28).

So it goes down the line. Angels with greater endowment have a greater obligation to serve. On earth, says Saint Denis, this principle is reflected in the Church's hierarchy. That is why the popes since Saint Gregory the Great have called themselves the "Servant of the Servants of God."

So the *more* powerful are constantly lifting up the *less* powerful, bringing them to a greater perfection. Denis continues:

> For all who have been called into the hierarchy find their perfection in being borne, in their own proper degree, to the imitation of God—and, what is most divine of all, they become "God's fellow workers" (Eph 3:9), as the Scriptures say, manifesting in themselves, as much as possible, the work of God.
>
> For it is the law of the hierarchy that some are purified while others purify. Some are enlightened while others enlighten. Some are perfected while others perfect. The imitation of God will suit each one in this fashion. The divine happiness, to use human terms, is something unstained by dissimilarity, and it is full of invisible light. It is perfect and lacks no perfection. It is cleansing, enlightening, and perfecting....

What is more, those who purify should give, from their own overflowing purity, their own proper holiness. Those who illuminate have more luminous intelligence, and it is their task to receive and to bestow light. And they are joyful and filled with holy gladness that these gifts should overflow, in proportion to their own overflowing light, toward those who are worthy to be enlightened. Those who perfect others are skilled in bestowing perfection, and they should indeed perfect those in their charge, through their sacred teaching, in the knowledge and contemplation of holy things.

Thus each rank of the hierarchical order is led, in its own degree, to be co-workers with God. By grace and God-given power, it does things that are naturally and supernaturally proper to God, things accomplished by Him transcendently, and manifested in the hierarchy, for the attainable imitation of the God-loving minds.[4]

God did not *need* to create. He is self-sufficient. Yet in the superabundance of his love he created a cosmos to reflect that love and accomplish that love. Love is the reason for the hierarchy. The greater love serves and lifts up the lesser.

So what do we know about the angelic hierarchy? We see angels frequently in Scripture acting as messengers of God. Archangels have special missions—either to deliver earthshakingly important messages (like, "You will conceive in your womb and bear a son, and you shall call his name Jesus") or to lead the fight against the powers of darkness.

Scripture tells us little about the other levels—except in the case of the cherubim.

PROTECTORS OF HOLY PLACES

The cherubim act as guardians of holy places, starting with the
Garden of Eden after Adam and Eve were expelled:

> Then the LORD God said, "Behold, the man has become like
> one of us, knowing good and evil; and now, lest he put forth
> his hand and take also of the tree of life, and eat, and live for
> ever"—therefore the LORD God sent him forth from the gar-
> den of Eden, to till the ground from which he was taken. He
> drove out the man; and at the east of the garden of Eden he
> placed the cherubim, and a flaming sword which turned every
> way, to guard the way to the tree of life. (Genesis 3:22–24)

When Moses had the ark of the covenant built, he was
instructed to carve two cherubim as the symbolic guardians of
the Lord's throne. "Of one piece with the mercy seat shall you
make the cherubim on its two ends. The cherubim shall spread
out their wings above, overshadowing the mercy seat with their
wings, their faces one to another; toward the mercy seat shall the
faces of the cherubim be" (Exodus 25:19–20).

There were also cherubim woven into the curtains of the
tabernacle and into the veil that separated the holy place from
the Holy of Holies, where the ark of the covenant rested:

> Moreover you shall make the tabernacle with ten curtains
> of fine twined linen and blue and purple and scarlet stuff;
> with cherubim skilfully worked shall you make them.
> (Exodus 26:1)

> And you shall make a veil of blue and purple and scarlet stuff
> and fine twined linen; in skilled work shall it be made, with
> cherubim; and you shall hang it upon four pillars of acacia

overlaid with gold, with hooks of gold, upon four bases of
silver. And you shall hang the veil from the clasps, and bring
the ark of the covenant in there within the veil; and the veil
shall separate for you the holy place from the most holy. You
shall put the mercy seat upon the ark of the covenant in the
most holy place. (Exodus 26:31–34)

When Solomon built the temple, cherubim again figured
prominently as guardians of the holy places:

In the inner sanctuary he made two cherubim of olivewood,
each ten cubits high. Five cubits was the length of one wing of
the cherub, and five cubits the length of the other wing of the
cherub; it was ten cubits from the tip of one wing to the tip
of the other. The other cherub also measured ten cubits; both
cherubim had the same measure and the same form.... He
put the cherubim in the innermost part of the house; and the
wings of the cherubim were spread out so that a wing of one
touched the one wall, and a wing of the other cherub touched
the other wall; their other wings touched each other in the
middle of the house. (1 Kings 6:23–25, 27)

A cubit is about half a meter or yard, so these cherubim were
about fifteen feet high, with wings as broad as they were tall.

The mercy seat on the ark of the covenant was God's throne
among his people; it was a reflection of his heavenly throne,
where he sat "enthroned upon the cherubim" (Psalm 80:1). The
prophet Ezekiel had a vivid vision of those cherubim forming a
kind of chariot for God's throne in heaven:

Then I looked, and behold, on the firmament that was over
the heads of the cherubim there appeared above them something like a sapphire, in form resembling a throne....

And I looked, and behold, there were four wheels beside the cherubim, one beside each cherub; and the appearance of the wheels was like sparkling chrysolite. And as for their appearance, the four had the same likeness, as if a wheel were within a wheel. When they went, they went in any of their four directions without turning as they went, but in whatever direction the front wheel faced the others followed without turning as they went. And their rims, and their spokes, and the wheels were full of eyes round about—the wheels that the four of them had. As for the wheels, they were called in my hearing the whirling wheels. And every one had four faces: the first face was the face of the cherub, and the second face was the face of a man, and the third the face of a lion, and the fourth the face of an eagle. (Ezekiel 10:1, 9–14)

As the book of Sirach tells us, "It was Ezekiel who saw the vision of glory which God showed him above the chariot of the cherubim" (Sirach 49:8). Ezekiel's vision is heavily symbolic, of course. We're not meant to suppose that cherubim really look like that, because as spirits they don't really *look* like anything to our eyes. But Ezekiel's description expresses power and instantaneous mobility by means of earthly images.

Meanwhile, farther down the hierarchy, there is one kind of angel we meet every day. In fact, these angels never leave us, even though, perhaps, we do not think about them as much as we should.

 GUARDIAN ANGELS

It is written, "He will give his angels charge of you,"
and "On their hands they will bear you up,
lest you strike your foot against a stone."
(Matthew 4:6)

. . . .

It certainly is written that way. Right there in the Old Testament, it says that God will give us angels to guard us. The text quoted in Matthew comes from Psalm 91, which seems to tell us that angels will keep us safe no matter how bad things get:

Because you have made the LORD your refuge,
　　the Most High your habitation,
no evil shall befall you,
　　no scourge come near your tent.

For he will give his angels charge of you
　　to guard you in all your ways.
On their hands they will bear you up,
　　lest you dash your foot against a stone.
You will tread on the lion and the adder,
　　the young lion and the serpent you will trample under foot.
(Psalm 91:9–13)

Our guardian angels are with us all the time; Scripture tells us so. This certainly isn't the only passage either.

"The angel of the LORD encamps / around those who fear him, and delivers them," says Psalm 34:7.

Jesus warns us, "See that you do not despise one of these little ones; for I tell you that in heaven their angels always behold the face of my Father who is in heaven" (Matthew 18:10).

The faithful, in fact, have always believed in a particular angel for each person. When Peter escaped from prison (with an angel's help), his friends couldn't believe it was really Peter at the door. "It is his angel" seemed like a more reasonable explanation (Acts 12:15).

The early Fathers of the Church were unanimous in their belief in guardian angels. We find testimony in Saint Clement of Alexandria (AD 195), his countryman Origen (AD 225), Saint Gregory the Wonderworker (AD 255) and Saint Methodius (AD 290). That's just a sampling from the years before Christianity was legal. In the next century the great Scripture scholar Saint Jerome wrote: "How great the dignity of the soul, since each one has from his birth an angel commissioned to guard it."[1]

But if there really are guardian angels, why do bad things happen? If it's true that "on their hands they will bear you up, lest you dash your foot against a stone," then why did I stub my toe just yesterday?

Look more closely at that verse from Matthew at the top of this chapter. It's the *devil* who quoted Psalm 91!

> Then the devil took him to the holy city, and set him on the pinnacle of the temple, and said to him, "If you are the Son of God, throw yourself down; for it is written,

'He will give his angels charge of you,'

and

   'On their hands they will bear you up,

   lest you strike your foot against a stone.'" (Matthew 4:5–6)

Jesus put Satan in his place with another piece of Scripture: "Again it is written, 'You shall not tempt the Lord your God'" (Matthew 4:7). It seems that we're expected to do a bit of looking out for ourselves.

But if guardian angels aren't keeping us from stubbing our toes, what are they doing? Why do we have them in the first place?

The answer is that *physical* harm is less important than spiritual harm from the heavenly perspective.

The Real Job of Guardian Angels

Our guardian angel's task is to get us to heaven. We often forget this. We tend to think of guardian angels as they appear on holy cards—pulling children back from a precipice, guiding them over a rickety bridge. There's something to this, of course. No doubt many people have discovered the doctrine of the guardian angels while sitting in a foxhole losing their eardrums to exploding munitions. But that's quite secondary.

Our guardian angel's task is to get us to heaven—not to keep us or our loved ones from suffering or death. After all, suffering is perhaps the principal means of our spiritual growth on earth, and death is our final portal to God.

We should not be surprised when friends, or even children, die in accidents. Nor should we see it as some sort of angelic malfunction. The angel's job is to get his charge to judgment, prepared as well as possible. The angels live in the presence of God, and they know God's mind better than we do. They know when an injury or illness will draw us closer to God. They also

47

know when another twenty-four hours on earth will merely get us another day older and deeper in debt.

God permits our suffering and even our death, always for the good of souls—for our own soul, if we correspond to the grace, for the good of others if we don't. The angels always cooperate with his perfect plan.

Judged from a human perspective, this can seem cold and even cruel. But the human perspective is limited. It takes an exceptionally talented human mind to see beyond it.

The novelist Muriel Spark wrote darkly humorous stories that disturbed some readers, who thought that Christians shouldn't joke about suffering. She told *The New Yorker*, "People say my novels are cruel because cruel things happen and I keep this even tone." But Spark was trying to give an angel-eye view: "There's a moral statement too, and what it's saying is that there's a life beyond this, and these events are not the most important things. They're not important in the long run."[2]

That's the angelic perspective. This life and its aches and accidents, troubles and trials, take their ultimate value from the "life beyond this." The angels want us to do right by our souls. And if we choose to disregard them, and disregard God, then they will try to minimize the damage we do to others.

Nevertheless, through most of our time here, we will stand in need of much more time here—to draw still closer to God and prepare ourselves for judgment. That's the reason why our angels will sometimes go to extraordinary lengths to keep us safe.

THERE WHEN WE NEED THEM

Even though angels see things from the heavenly perspective, we shouldn't think of them as indifferent to our everyday concerns.

God himself does not despise our wishes for cures and safety, wisdom and courage. He even went to the extreme of becoming human in order to alleviate these anxieties and pains by his touch. Often he uses his angels for this purpose.

Our guardian angel sympathizes with our desire to find a parking space and will likely help—unless that parking space might detour us on the way to heaven. Sometimes, after all, we're better off being late for an appointment. This side of Judgment Day, we won't know when those "sometimes" occur.

We should have no doubt that angels do intervene for us, sometimes very directly.

A friend of mine, a noted Harvard-trained philosopher, was an unbeliever as a young man. One day he was swimming in the ocean, and the undertow swept him away. He knew he was drowning, with no hope of rescue, when suddenly a strong arm grabbed him and towed him to shore. His rescuer was a big muscle-bound guy. When my sputtering friend tried to thank him, the guy laughed at him—and then vanished. This marked a milestone on my friend's road to conversion.

Another friend of mine, the veteran journalist Phil Taylor, wrote a heartrending reminiscence of the early 1960s, when his parents enrolled him, at age six, as the first African American student in his school. Integration was quite a burden for a kid in kindergarten. Little Phil withstood the taunts and beatings as much as he could. But one day he just couldn't stand it any longer.

Phil ran out of the school in what he thought was the direction of his home. He ran hard, and he kept running until he found himself beside a busy six-lane expressway:

I had made a wrong turn and continued on the wrong course.

I stood there in frigid weather, watching the cars whiz by at 50 or 60 miles per hour. I thought if the stream of traffic slowed and I ran fast enough, I could get to the other side. The truth is that my small body would have been smashed and tossed by vehicle after vehicle.

As I tensed, my muscles preparing to make a go of it, an elderly woman's hand locked onto my shoulder. I remember vaguely that she was black and small and wore the same kind of clothes my grandmother wore. She asked me what I was doing. I told her. She said I would have been killed.

The woman consoled me, as if she knew what was really going on inside me. I told her everything...but she seemed to already know. She took me home and then...disappeared. She had intervened and saved my life. Was she my guardian angel?[3]

There is, of course, no way of knowing this side of heaven.

A saint of the twentieth century, Josemaría Escrivá, lived through the Spanish Civil War, a horrible time when the country was split between the Hitler-supported Fascists and the socialists, who persecuted the Catholic faith and made martyrs of many priests, nuns and laypeople. Francis Fernandez tells the story of one narrow escape Father Josemaría had:

Once during a time of intense anticlerical persecution in Madrid a would-be aggressor stood menacingly in Josemaría's path with the obvious intention of doing him harm. Someone suddenly stood between them and drove off the assailant. It all happened in an instant. The protector came up after the incident and whispered to him: "Mangy donkey, mangy donkey," the expression Blessed Josemaría used to refer to himself in the intimacy of his soul. Only his confessor knew about this. Peace and joy filled his heart as he recognized the intervention of his Angel.[4]

Flannery O'Connor, the famous storyteller, remembered a very close relationship with her own guardian angel—but certainly not a cordial one.

> I went to the Sisters to school for the first 6 years or so... at their hands I developed something the Freudians have not named—anti-angel aggression, call it. From 8 to 12 years it was my habit to seclude myself in a locked room every so often and with a fierce (and evil) face, whirl round in a circle with my fists knotted, socking the angel. This was the guardian angel with which the Sisters assured us we were all equipped. He never left you. My dislike of him was poisonous. I'm sure I even kicked at him and landed on the floor. You couldn't hurt an angel but I would have been happy to know I had dirtied his feathers.... Anyway, the Lord removed this fixation from me by His Merciful Kindness and I have not been troubled by it since.[5]

GUARDIANS OF THE NATIONS

Guardians are just as important for institutions as they are for individuals. In Revelation, when John was given messages for the seven churches in Asia, he was told to write "to the angel of the church" in each city. Origen called these angels the churches' "invisible" bishops.[6]

Every nation has its own angel as well:

> When the Most High gave to the nations their inheritance,
>   when he separated the sons of men,
> he fixed the bounds of the peoples

according to the number of the sons of God.

(Deuteronomy 32:8)

"Sons of God" is usually interpreted as "angels," and indeed the Septuagint, the ancient Greek version of the Old Testament that the earliest Christians used, translated "sons of God" as "angels of God."

Saint Gregory the Great tells us that even the angels come into conflict when nations are in conflict:

> But because there are fixed charges of the angels set to super-intend the regulating of the several particular nations, when the practices of the subject peoples deserve the assistance of the presiding spirits against one another, the spirits them-selves that are set in charge are said to come against one another.... Therefore it is rightly said that the angels come against each other, because the claims of the nations under them are reciprocally at odds with one another. *For the lofty spirits that are princes to those nations never fight in behalf of those that act unjustly, but justly judge and try their deeds.* And when either the guilt or guiltlessness of each separate nation is brought into the debate of the court above, the ruling spirit of that nation is said to have won in the conflict or not to have won; the one identical victory of all of whom, however, is the supreme will of their Maker above them, which will whilst they ever have before their eyes, what they have not the power they have not the mind to obtain.[7]

Does this mean that, when nations are at war, their angels are at war too? Of course not. Rather Gregory makes the point that the angels "justly judge and try their deeds." The guardians of the nations are always at work as advocates for their charges.

Get the Most From Your Guardian Angel

So if we know that there really are guardian angels, what do we do with that knowledge? What should it mean to us?

First, the example of Jesus' temptation teaches us that we shouldn't take stupid chances and expect our guardian angels to keep us out of trouble. The guardian angels do what they can, but we have free will. If we decide to do something really stupid, the guardian angels may defer to our decision.

But if we sincerely want to do the right thing, the angels can help us. So we should cultivate a devotion to the guardian angels. They're powerful spiritual beings who want us to succeed at being good. They want us to end up in heaven.

Just remembering that our guardian angels are always there is a good way to keep ourselves on the right path. We tend to behave better when we know someone's watching. And our angels are always watching.

Our angels can be immensely helpful too in everyday life. We can call upon our own angel as well as the angels of those around us—our family members, coworkers, neighbors and even our adversaries. (The Back of the Book includes some traditional prayers to the angels. Try them out!)

If you're married, for example, it's useful to know that your spouse's angel wants you to succeed in creating a happy home. You can ask for the help of your honey's angel.

If you're a parent, it's helpful to keep in mind that your children have guardian angels, and those angels want you to succeed at parenting. So when you're beginning to lose patience, ask your own guardian angel to help you. If the situation keeps getting worse, call on your kids' guardian angels as well. In fact, the system works best if you greet each child's angel (silently, in your heart) each time the child strolls into your presence.

Saint Josemaría suggested that guardian angels can be a big help in evangelization too. "Win over the guardian angel of the one you want to draw to your apostolate. He is always a great 'accomplice.'"[8]

Think of all the people who most need your Christian witness: a son or daughter? a son-in-law? a daughter-in-law? an estranged friend? a former colleague? What's the best way to begin to reach them? Well, each of them has a guardian angel who's eager to help!

The main thing is to be aware of the angels around you—and get in the habit of calling upon them for little favors. Invoke them silently as you begin each conversation, as you dial the phone, as you start to reply to an e-mail. Ask them to give you the right words. Ask them to help you avoid words that can damage your relationships and compromise your Christian witness.

And don't stop asking the angels to keep you safe and healthy! Go ahead and call upon your angel every time you start your car or cross a busy street. We can't help but be self-interested; it's our nature. But grace builds on nature. If our natural desire for safety brings heavenly assistance ever to our minds, that's a very good thing. It builds a habit of drawing near to the angels, and that's a habit that can only help us as we go through life and face other perils: temptations to immorality, temptations against faith, temptations to say hurtful things.

Our angels are *always* there, *always* doing their best to keep us on the path to heaven. But there's one place in particular where Christians meet the angels—and meet them as equals.

THE ANGELS AT WORSHIP

. . .

I*f angels are everywhere—and indeed they are—they're all over the Mass.*
So preached Saint John Chrysostom in an Ascension Day
homily: "The angels are present here. The angels and the martyrs gather here today. If you want to see the angels and martyrs,
open the eyes of faith and look upon this scene. *For if the air itself
is filled with angels, so much more the Church!*"[1]

Old Testament worship was an imitation of the heavenly
liturgy, and the earthly sanctuaries were constructed according to
heavenly prototypes. Moses received the plans for the tabernacle
straight from heaven (see Exodus 25:9). When Solomon built the
temple, he followed the same pattern, which he had received
from his father David (see 1 Chronicles 28:11–13). The Wisdom
of Solomon points out that the pattern of the temple was the
same as the pattern of the tabernacle—"a copy of the holy tent
which you prepared from the beginning" (Wisdom 9:8).

As the throne of the Lord was guarded by cherubim in
heaven, the holiest part of the tabernacle and the temple was
guarded by carved cherubim. Cherubim were also embroidered
in the fabric decorations. The tabernacle, and later the temple,
was an imitation of the heavenly court.

In the New Testament, though, we move beyond imitation. Though we still live on earth, our real home is in heaven.

> But you have come to Mount Zion and to the city of the living God, the heavenly Jerusalem, and to innumerable angels in festal gathering, and to the assembly of the first-born who are enrolled in heaven, and to a judge who is God of all, and to the spirits of just men made perfect, and to Jesus, the mediator of a new covenant, and to the sprinkled blood that speaks more graciously than the blood of Abel. (Hebrews 12:22–24)

When we walk into a church where the Mass is going on—and it doesn't matter how tiny or huge the church is, or whether it's filled with masterpieces of art or with bland mass-produced decorations, or whether we hear a choir singing perfect harmony or one tone-deaf old priest—we walk straight into heaven.

My friend Scott Hahn expresses it better than I ever could:

> The people of ancient Israel considered their earthly liturgy to be a divinely inspired imitation of heavenly worship.... Yet it was still only a shadow of the angels' worship—and only a shadow of the earthly worship that would be inaugurated in the age of the Messiah.
>
> By assuming human flesh, the eternal Son of God brought heaven to earth. No longer must the People of God worship in imitation of angels. In the liturgy of the New Covenant, Christ Himself presides and we not only imitate the angels, we participate with them.[2]

Participating With the Angels

Very early in the Mass, in the *Confiteor*, we confess the angels' presence: "I ask...all the angels and saints, and you my brothers and sisters, to pray for me to the Lord our God."

And the rites grow still more angelic from there. Some of the songs of the Mass are the angels' hymns. There's the *Gloria*, which the angels sang at the first Christmas: "Glory to God in the highest" (Luke 2:14). And then "Holy, holy, holy is the LORD of hosts; / the whole earth is full of his glory"—that was the hymn of the seraphim in Isaiah's vision of the heavenly court (Isaiah 6:3). Read that sixth chapter of Isaiah, and you'll notice that the seraphim were singing responsively—just as we do in the responsorial psalm in the Mass today. "And one called to another and said: 'Holy, holy, holy'" (Isaiah 6:3).

The historian Socrates Scholasticus, who wrote in the fifth century, tells us that it was a first-century bishop, Saint Ignatius, who started the custom of responsive singing in the Christian churches—and he had angelic reasons for doing so:

> Ignatius [was the] third bishop of Antioch in Syria after the apostle Peter, and he conversed with the apostles themselves. Once he saw a vision of angels hymning in alternate chants the Holy Trinity. Accordingly he introduced the mode of singing he had observed in the vision into the Antiochian church; whence it was transmitted by tradition to all the other churches.[3]

Saint Ignatius, it seems, had the same kind of vision that Isaiah had: angelic beings, one calling to another.

So when we sing in the Mass, we worship God in the same way the angels have always done. That's an astonishing thing if you think about it. We're not just earthbound mortals anymore. In the liturgy we become part of the angelic choir. We're swept right up into heaven with the angels, singing praise to God alongside them. It doesn't even matter if we're tone-deaf: The liturgy puts us in God's court with the seraphim.

This is not hyperbole. In the Mass, Saint John Chrysostom tells us, "man is as it were transported into heaven itself. He stands near the throne of glory. He flies with the Seraphim. He sings the most holy hymn."[4]

The early Christians not only believed that they were participating in the liturgy of the angels, but some of them literally sensed the presence of the angels in their own churches. Chrysostom tells two stories:

[During the Mass] angels stand by the priest; and the whole sanctuary, and the space round about the altar, is filled with the powers of heaven, in honor of him who lies on the altar....

I myself heard someone once tell of a certain old, venerable man, who was accustomed to see revelations.... At such a time, he suddenly saw, as far as was possible for him, a multitude of angels, clothed in shining robes, encircling the altar, and bending down, as soldiers might in the presence of their king. And for my part I believe it.

Moreover another man told me—without learning it from someone else, but as himself an eyewitness—that those who are about to depart from this world, and who have received the sacraments with a pure conscience, are guarded by angels when they draw their last breath. And for the sake of what they have received, the angels bear them away.[5]

We hear the angels mentioned throughout the Mass. Many, if not most, of the Prefaces invoke the angels' participation. "Through [Christ] the angels and all the choirs of heaven worship in awe before your presence. May our voices be one with theirs as they sing."

Here is where we join the angel chorus; we sing the hymns the angels sing. And we eat the bread of angels.

PANIS ANGELICUS

The manna that the Israelites ate in the wilderness was called "the bread of angels" by the sacred writers:

> Yet he commanded the skies above,
>> and opened the doors of heaven;
> and he rained down upon them manna to eat,
>> and gave them the bread of heaven.
> Man ate of the bread of the angels;
>> he sent them food in abundance. (Psalm 78:23–25)

> Instead of these things you gave your people
>> the food of angels,
> and without their toil you supplied them from
>> heaven with bread ready to eat,
> providing every pleasure and suited to every
>> taste. (Wisdom 16:20)

The rabbis continued to refer to the historic manna as "angels' bread." And they added that, in the coming age, the Messiah would feed his people with manna, the bread of the angels, which would make God's chosen people "mighty as angels."[6]

We live in the age of the Messiah. We feed on the bread of angels. We indeed are made mighty as angels!

In the New Testament Paul recalls the manna in the wilderness:

> I want you to know, brethren, that our fathers were all under the cloud, and all passed through the sea, and all were baptized into Moses in the cloud and in the sea, and all ate the same supernatural food and all drank the same supernatural drink. For they drank from the supernatural Rock which followed them, and the Rock was Christ. (1 Corinthians 10:1–4)

Paul compares the manna to the Eucharist that Christians celebrate. "Because there is one bread, we who are many are one body, for we all partake of the one bread" (1 Corinthians 10:17).

Eucharistic Prayer I asks, "Almighty God, / we pray that your angel may take this sacrifice / to your altar in heaven."[7] Traditional Catholic hymns speak of the Eucharist as "angelic bread" and "bread of angels." Think of the sublime *Panis Angelicus* and *O Esca Viatorum, O Panis Angelorum* ("O Food of Men Wayfaring, O Bread of Angels").

The angels dwell in the presence of God, and we can't imagine what that's like. But then we think a moment and realize that we too dwell in the presence of God. Not just because God is omnipresent but because we actually touch and taste the Body of Christ. We are as close to God as the angels are.

Perhaps even closer. Perhaps this is one of those things into which angels long to look.

 Michael, Our Defender

. . . .

I bear his name. *He is patron of my ancestral city, Caltanissetta, Sicily. In* the East his memorial is my birthday.

All of this is coincidental. I was named after my dad. But even reckoning without me personally, there are many other reasons why Michael should be important to this book, to its author and to you readers.

The name of Michael is first ascribed to an individual angel in the book of Daniel. We've already looked at Daniel's description of his angel visions: "His body was like beryl, his face like the appearance of lightning, his eyes like flaming torches, his arms and legs like the gleam of burnished bronze, and the sound of his words like the noise of a multitude" (Daniel 10:6). This frightening being, whom some commentators identify as Gabriel, came with a message for Daniel:

> Fear not, Daniel, for from the first day that you set your mind
> to understand and humbled yourself before your God, your
> words have been heard, and I have come because of your
> words. The prince of the kingdom of Persia withstood me
> twenty-one days; but Michael, one of the chief princes, came
> to help me, so I left him there with the prince of the kingdom
> of Persia and came to make you understand what is to befall

your people in the latter days. For the vision is for days yet to come. (Daniel 10:12–14)

This is a strange thing to say, and a bit confusing to modern ears. The angel was filling in a bit of what we might call back story. He came in answer to Daniel's prayers, but he was delayed along the way because he was fighting against the "prince"—the angelic guardian—of Persia. Only when Michael showed up could he spare the time to visit Daniel.

And who is this Michael? "But I will tell you what is inscribed in the book of truth: there is none who contends by my side against these except Michael, your prince" (Daniel 10:21). Michael is "your prince"—the angelic guardian of Israel.

DEFENDER OF ISRAEL

Daniel's angelic visitor went on to reveal a history of the future in figurative language—a history filled with wars between great empires, in which the people of Israel would be pawns and would be sorely tempted to deny their God. But just when things looked worst, Michael would be on their side:

At that time shall arise Michael, the great prince who has charge of your people. And there shall be a time of trouble, such as never has been since there was a nation till that time; but at that time your people shall be delivered, every one whose name shall be found written in the book. And many of those who sleep in the dust of the earth shall awake, some to everlasting life, and some to shame and everlasting contempt. And those who are wise shall shine like the brightness of the firmament; and those who turn many to righteousness, like the stars for ever and ever. (Daniel 12:1–3)

Michael, protector of Israel, will keep the faithful safe through the time of tribulation.

This is Michael's role in Scripture and in Christian tradition as well. Michael's name means "Who is like God?"—the battle cry of the angels on God's side. His motto is "I will serve"—a direct repudiation of the rebellion of Satan. When the forces of evil mass against the people of God, Michael fights on the side of good, leading the angelic hosts to victory.

It's not surprising then that some interpreters have identified Michael as the mysterious "commander" Joshua encountered on his approach to Jericho.

> When Joshua was by Jericho, he lifted up his eyes and looked, and behold, a man stood before him with his drawn sword in his hand; and Joshua went to him and said to him, "Are you for us, or for our adversaries?" And he said, "No; but as commander of the army of the LORD I have now come." And Joshua fell on his face to the earth, and worshiped, and said to him, "What does my lord bid his servant?" And the commander of the LORD's army said to Joshua, "Put off your shoes from your feet; for the place where you stand is holy." And Joshua did so. (Joshua 5:13–15)

Certainly this appearance matches Michael's role as explained by the angel in Daniel, and this scene has obviously influenced iconography of Michael.

The Letter of Jude refers to another ancient story, not written in the Old Testament but passed down through Jewish tradition: "But when the archangel Michael, contending with the devil, disputed about the body of Moses, he did not presume to pronounce a reviling judgment upon him, but said, 'The Lord rebuke you'" (Jude 1:9).

In the ancient story Satan contended that Moses did not deserve a proper burial, since he had been a murderer (see Exodus 2:11–12). Though Satan did his best to provoke Michael, Michael never fell to the temptation to use intemperate language—unlike, Jude says, the false teachers who wanted to lead the Church astray.

Both the rabbis and the Fathers were alert to find Michael throughout the Old Testament. He is, in ancient sources, identified with most of the appearances of angels in Genesis: guarding Eden, halting Abraham's sacrifice of Isaac, wrestling with Jacob and so on. (Michael also appears once in the Koran, and Muslim interpretive tradition finds him in several biblical scenes—notably that of Abraham's three visitors.)

Since Michael is the protector of God's chosen people, Satan himself is Michael's opponent. Revelation tells us that Michael led the armies of God against the evil angels: "Now war arose in heaven, Michael and his angels fighting against the dragon; and the dragon and his angels fought, but they were defeated and there was no longer any place for them in heaven" (Revelation 12:7–8).

As for Michael's rank in the hierarchy, much depends upon how one reads the hierarchies. He's usually called an "archangel," but that could refer to a specific rank or a priority over all the angels.

Whatever his rank—and whatever rank even means to angels—it was clear to the early Christians that they had in Michael a powerful protector. The protector of Israel continues his work in guarding God's Church.

THE CHURCH'S PROTECTOR

Michael's appeal in the first centuries of the Church must have been tremendous: He was a warrior and defender for a persecuted minority, a vanquisher of demons in a world that seemed demon-possessed, a defender of Moses' relics at a time when the pagans abused the corpses of the saints.

Naturally enough, then, devotion to Saint Michael came early. Some of the first churches named were named for Michael, in lands as far-flung as Egypt and Rome. Beginning in the era of the Fathers, apparitions of Michael have been reported throughout Christian history. One of the most famous appearances gave a name to one of Rome's best-known landmarks.

Rome in the year 589 was a broken city. It had never quite recovered from the barbarian invasions and the years of civil war that followed. But in 589 came a devastating flood, and after that a pestilence that took the lives of countless citizens—among them Pope Pelagius.

According to legend, amid the great plague in 590, Gregory the Great led a penitential procession through the city. As the procession passed the mausoleum of the Emperor Hadrian, Michael appeared atop it, sheathing his sword as a sign that the plague was ended. Here is how the Golden Legend, the famous medieval compilation of holy lore, tells the story:

> The third apparition [of Michael] happened in the time of
> Gregory the pope. For when the said pope had established
> the litanies for the pestilence that was at that time, and
> prayed devoutly for the people, he saw upon the castle which
> was called the castle in memory of Hadrian, the angel of God,
> who wiped and made clean a bloody sword, and put it into a

sheath. And thereby he understood that his prayers were heard. Then he had a church established there in honor of St. Michael, and that castle is still called the Castle Angel.[1]

"Castle Angel" is an English name for what we today know as *Castel Sant'Angelo*. It is one of Rome's great monuments, situated not far from St. Peter's Square. From its forecourts the justly famous "Angel Bridge" spans the Tiber River. The angels that flank the walkway hold the instruments of Jesus' Passion.

The story in the Golden Legend was probably set down between 950 and 1150, but it was based on an ancient tradition, whose details are confirmed by many historical sources. There was a flood and a plague in 590, and Michael was indeed honored as patron of the fortress from the time of Pope Gregory. And we know that there was a chapel at the top of the *castellum* (in the one-time funerary chamber of Emperor Hadrian), at least from the time of Gregory's near successor, Pope Boniface IV, who served from 608 to 615.

And Gregory himself went on record, preaching: "Whenever some act of wondrous power must be performed, Michael is sent, so that his action and his name may make it clear that no one can do what God does by his superior power."[2]

DEFEND US IN BATTLE

One morning in the late 1800s, while attending a Mass of thanksgiving, Pope Leo XIII started acting very odd. The people around him saw him lift his head and stare at something above the celebrant—something no one else could see. He sat transfixed and stared, and his expression attested to the fact that he was seeing something horrible.

After some time Pope Leo stood up and marched toward his

office. The retinue followed quickly, murmuring. Was the Holy Father all right? Did he need anything? Yes, he answered shortly, he was fine; no, he didn't need anything.

Within half an hour the pope called for the secretary of rites and handed him a sheet of paper, with orders to send a copy to every bishop in the world. On that sheet of paper was the Prayer to Saint Michael:

Saint Michael the Archangel, defend us in battle.
  Be our protection against the wickedness and snares of the devil;
  May God rebuke him, we humbly pray.
  And do thou, O prince of the heavenly host,
  by the power of God,
  cast into hell Satan and all evil spirits
  who prowl through the world seeking the ruin of souls.
  Amen.

What had Pope Leo seen?

His secretary said that it was a vision of evil spirits gathering at Rome. He added that people at the Vatican often heard Pope Leo reciting that prayer to Saint Michael. Other stories—less reliable but more detailed—tell how Pope Leo saw Satan himself negotiating with God for more control over the world in the twentieth century.

Whatever the particulars were, Pope Leo obviously thought it very important that people all over the world call on Saint Michael to defend us. The Saint Michael Prayer is still very popular among Catholics, and there's no doubt that the faithful can use a strong protector today, just as in Pope Leo's day—or Pope Gregory's day.

Saint Michael has two feasts on the Church's calendar. May 8 marks a sixth-century apparition on Mount Gargano in southern Italy. At that time the angel asked that a church be built there. Chips of rock from the cave where he appeared are often distributed as "relics" of the angel. (I have a friend, a Franciscan priest, who carries such a relic with him.)

Saint Michael's main feast, September 29, which he now shares with the other archangels, Raphael and Gabriel, has been an important holiday, socially as well as liturgically, since at least the Middle Ages. "Michaelmas" was a time for celebrating the harvest and sharing a goose with family and neighbors. Many European schools still begin their fall semester on that day, and that semester is known as "Michaelmas Term."

Saint Michael is patron of many groups, places, professions and activities, most famously EMTs, police officers and soldiers but also bankers and dying people. Until 1970 the prayers in the liturgy addressed him as the angel who presented the soul for judgment.

In art Michael is often portrayed with Satan beneath his feet. He holds a sword and sometimes a banner. Often the banner is emblazoned with the Latin word *serviam*—a reversal of Satan's refusal to serve but also a succinct statement of the basic principle of the heavenly hierarchy, which is loving service.

Sometimes too Michael is depicted with the scales of judgment, and so he has been called "The Weigher." (See James Russell Lowell's poem by that name at the Back of the Book.)

GABRIEL, THE GREAT COMMUNICATOR

When I, Daniel, had seen the vision, I sought to understand it; and behold, there stood before me one having the appearance of a man. And I heard a man's voice between the banks of the Ulai, and it called, "Gabriel, make this man understand the vision." So he came near where I stood; and when he came, I was frightened and fell upon my face. But he said to me, "Understand, O son of man, that the vision is for the time of the end." (Daniel 8:15–17)

. . . . . .

T*his is where we first meet Gabriel by name in the Bible. Daniel had* a strange and shocking vision, and Gabriel was the one to explain it.

The name Gabriel means "God is my strength" or "the strength of God," and his special mission seems to be communicating the gospel. That's what Daniel's vision signified. In figures and symbols Daniel had been shown the future—a future that would climax in the "Prince of princes," the Messiah.

I AM GABRIEL

Flash forward to the New Testament, where the prophetic visions granted to Daniel reach their fulfillment. Once more Gabriel brought the Good News. We meet him in the Gospel of Luke, where he came first to Zechariah, an old priest, to tell him that—in spite of his own age and his wife's advanced years—he would have a son, who

> will turn many of the sons of Israel to the Lord their God,
> and...will go before him in the spirit and power of Elijah,
> to turn the hearts of the fathers to the children,
> and the disobedient to the wisdom of the just,
> to make ready for the Lord a people prepared. (Luke 1:16–17)

It's the beginning of the Gospel story. The son would be John the Baptist, whose mission was to prepare the way for the Messiah.

Zechariah asked, naturally enough, how he could be sure that his wife and he could have a child at such an advanced age.

"I am Gabriel," the angel answered, "who stand in the presence of God; and I was sent to speak to you, and to bring you this good news" (Luke 1:19). Bringing good news is Gabriel's job.

Of all the angels it is Gabriel who is most closely associated with the coming of the Messiah. His next appearance in Luke is without a doubt the best-known angelic appearance in the Bible.

> "It was only fitting that the highest angel should come to announce the greatest of all messages," wrote Saint Gregory the Great. "So too Gabriel, who is called God's strength, was sent to Mary. He came to announce the One who appeared as a humble man to quell the cosmic powers. Thus God's

strength announced the coming of the Lord of the heavenly powers, mighty in battle."[1]

You've heard the story countless times; I quoted it myself in chapter four. But hear it again, and this time try to see it from the point of view of the angel:

In the sixth month the angel Gabriel was sent from God to a city of Galilee named Nazareth, to a virgin betrothed to a man whose name was Joseph, of the house of David; and the virgin's name was Mary. And he came to her and said, "Hail, full of grace, the Lord is with you!" But she was greatly troubled at the saying, and considered in her mind what sort of greeting this might be. And the angel said to her, "Do not be afraid, Mary, for you have found favor with God. And behold, you will conceive in your womb and bear a son, and you shall call his name Jesus.

He will be great, and will be called the Son of the Most High; and the Lord God will give to him the throne of his father David,

and he will reign over the house of Jacob for ever;

and of his kingdom there will be no end."

And Mary said to the angel, "How can this be, since I have no husband?" And the angel said to her,

"The Holy Spirit will come upon you,

and the power of the Most High will overshadow you;

therefore the child to be born will be called holy,

the Son of God.

And behold, your kinswoman Elizabeth in her old age has also conceived a son; and this is the sixth month with her who was called barren. For with God nothing will be impossible."

And Mary said, "Behold, I am the handmaid of the Lord; let it be to me according to your word." And the angel departed from her. (Luke 1:26–38)

Notice how Gabriel greeted Mary: "Hail, full of grace, the Lord is with you!" He showed Mary deference, as though he, the angel—archangel, in fact, if you want to pull rank—was in awe of a humble Jewish woman who was hardly more than a girl. You'd think he was talking to somebody important.

THE QUEEN OF THE ANGELS

Truly Gabriel was speaking with the "Queen of the Angels." By divine grace Mary, who looked like a perfectly ordinary Palestinian girl, had been kept immaculate, free from the stain of original sin since her conception. She would be the one to give birth to the Lord. She was the culmination of Israel. She was the Israelite who at last answered a perfect yes to all God's plans.

In John's vision in Revelation, Mary reigns exalted in heaven: "And a great sign appeared in heaven, a woman clothed with the sun, with the moon under her feet, and on her head a crown of twelve stars" (Revelation 12:1).

Stars in Revelation represent angels—remember that the "ancient serpent," Satan, "swept down a third of the stars of heaven" (Revelation 12:4). The woman clothed with the sun, the mother of the Messiah, is crowned with angels.

Christian tradition quite reasonably identifies Gabriel as the unnamed angel in several other scenes of Scripture. Thus the angel who visited Joseph repeatedly could well have been Gabriel, and Gabriel is sometimes identified as the angel who gave Jesus strength in the Garden of Gethsemane. Some Jewish traditions also name him as the angel who destroyed Sodom and Gomorrah (see Genesis 19:1–13) and brought judgment to the Assyrian army.

Since Gabriel's role as the bearer of important news is so prominent, he is the natural patron of broadcasters and all those in electronic media; of preachers, postal workers, diplomats and messengers. He is a patron of almost every profession with *tele* in the name: television, telecommunications, telegraphs and telephones. From his connection with the postal service, he is also (logically enough) the patron of stamp collectors.

Gabriel's liturgical memorial (formerly March 24) is now shared with the other archangels, Michael and Raphael, on September 29.

Chapter Ten

 RAPHAEL, FRIEND AND GUIDE

. . . . . .

The story of Raphael is something unique in the whole Bible. There are other stories where angels came disguised as humans, and there are other stories where angels protected or led one of God's faithful people. But in all those stories, the angel's appearance, however important, was brief. The angel showed up, delivered his message or did his job and then left.

Raphael is different. He stayed around for the whole story, and by the end he had become something more than an angel. He had become a friend.

MY FRIEND THE ANGEL

This idea of friendship with an angel is a bit odd on the face of it. Certainly the old pagan philosophers, like Aristotle and Cicero, would hardly have admitted the idea. Remember that in the Old Testament, angels were seen as superior to men. So how can two beings so obviously unequal be "friends"?

The only possible answer is that friendship with an angel actually lifts the human up to the angel's level. And this is what happened with Raphael and Tobias. Tobias began the story poor, persecuted and with only the dimmest prospects in life. He ended happy, prosperous and established in an ideal marriage.

Raphael's name means "God has healed" or "healer of God." Saint Gregory the Great related the name to the story: "Raphael means 'God's remedy,' for when he touched Tobit's eyes in order to cure him, he banished the darkness of his blindness. Thus, since he is to heal, he is rightly called God's remedy."[1]

Nothing like this friendship happens anywhere else in the Bible. Yet it prefigures the accounts of later Christian saints who spoke of their angels with warmth usually reserved for the closest of friends.

The book of Tobit is the story of a pious man in impossible circumstances who wanted nothing more than a good life for his son. That would not be too much to ask, unless you lived in exile in a pagan empire, where piety toward the true God was punishable by death. Tobit was among those exiled to Nineveh after the Assyrian conquest of Israel.

The author establishes the piety of Tobit right away:

> I would give my bread to the hungry and my clothing to the naked; and if I saw any one of my people dead and thrown out behind the wall of Nineveh, I would bury him. And if Sennacherib the king put to death any who came fleeing from Judea, I buried them secretly. (Tobit 1:17–18)

Unfortunately, it seems as though Tobit was a living example of the old proverb, "No good deed goes unpunished." Returning from burying one of Sennacharib's unfortunate victims, Tobit had to sleep in the courtyard overnight, for touching the dead body had made him ritually unclean.

> I did not know that there were sparrows on the wall and their fresh droppings fell into my open eyes and white films formed on my eyes. I went to physicians to be healed, but the

more they treated me with ointments, the more my vision was obscured by the white films. (Tobit 2:10)

Since Tobit was blind and unable to work, his wife had to do "women's work" to keep the family going. She was not too happy about it. "Where are your charities and your righteous deeds?" she asked bitterly (Tobit 2:14). You can't eat righteousness. Tobit was so depressed, he prayed to be allowed to die.

Meanwhile, over in Media, a young Israelite woman named Sarah was also thinking of killing herself. The demon Asmodeus killed every man she married on the wedding night. She was a virgin and a widow seven times over. Now who would marry her? Her own maids thought she'd been strangling the men. The only thing that kept her from hanging herself was remembering that her father, who had no other children, would be devastated.

So instead of killing herself, she prayed for help: "If it be not pleasing to you to take my life, command that respect be shown to me and pity be taken upon me, and that I hear reproach no more" (Tobit 3:15).

Her prayers and Tobit's were heard in heaven.

And Raphael was sent to heal the two of them: to scale away the white films of Tobit's eyes; to give Sarah the daughter of Raguel in marriage to Tobias the son of Tobit, and to bind Asmodeus the evil demon, because Tobias was entitled to possess her. (Tobit 3:17)

But the healing, the binding and the marriage didn't happen right away. Tobias and Sarah, who had no idea they were destined for each other, lived far apart, separated by highways so dangerous that Tobit had not dared to travel them even when he could see.

However, Tobit had business dealings in Media from his younger days. He still had quite a bit of money deposited with an old friend there. Thinking he might be about to die (after all, he had prayed for death), he gave his son Tobias a chapter of good advice and then revealed that there was money waiting for him if he could make it to Media. "Find a man to go with you," Tobit told his son, "and I will pay him wages as long as I live; and go and get the money" (Tobit 5:3).

Here is where the threads of the story begin to come together. We know that Tobias was destined to marry Sarah; we know that Sarah was in Media; we know that Tobias had to go to Media on another errand; and we know that God was sending the angel Raphael to put everything right. "So [Tobias] went to look for a man; and he found Raphael, who was an angel, but Tobias did not know it" (Tobit 5:4–6).

This is the sort of plot twist that makes good farce so delightful: It's completely unexpected yet utterly plausible at the same time. We probably expected that Raphael would come to Tobias; instead Tobias came looking for him. Raphael went along with the gag. He knew what Tobias didn't know: that this journey, which Tobias thought was only about money, would resolve the intractable problems of three faithful people of God.

So Tobias brought Raphael back to his father, who interrogated him a bit about his genealogy. After all, he didn't want to entrust his son to just anybody. Raphael gave him a satisfying story, and Tobit agreed to hire "Azarias," as Raphael called himself, to be his son's companion and guide on the dangerous journey. Raphael didn't drive a very hard bargain on the salary, but then he probably didn't need the money.

Tobias's mother strongly objected to the trip.

> Why have you sent our child away? Is he not the staff of our
> hands as he goes in and out before us? Do not add money to
> money, but consider it as rubbish as compared to our child.
> For the life that is given to us by the Lord is enough for us.
> (Tobit 5:17–19)

But Tobit, with no awareness of the irony, assured her, "Do not
worry, my sister; he will return safe and sound, and your eyes
will see him. For a good angel will go with him; his journey will
be successful, and he will come back safe and sound" (Tobit
5:20–21).

Happy Endings

So Tobias and Raphael and Tobias's dog set out for Media. On
their way they camped by the Tigris River, and Tobias was nearly
eaten by a monstrous fish. Raphael told him to catch that fish
and keep the heart, liver and gall—they would be useful later.

> As for the heart and liver, if a demon or evil spirit gives trou-
> ble to any one, you make a smoke from these before the man
> or woman, and that person will never be troubled again. And
> as for the gall, anoint with it a man who has white films in his
> eyes, and he will be cured. (Tobit 6:7–8)

We've already been introduced to someone with demon problems and someone else with white films in his eyes. Tobias did the
sensible thing and followed his companion's instructions.

As they approached the city where both the money and
Sarah were, Raphael revealed the other part of the plan. They
would be staying with Sarah's father, and Tobias was the one
who ought to marry Sarah. Tobias wasn't so sure about that—
he'd heard about the seven dead husbands, and he could already

see a big number *8* on his own forehead. But Raphael assured him that everything would be all right. In fact, he would be married that night.

What about the demon? The heart and liver of the fish would take care of that. Make a smoke from them, Raphael told Tobias, and the demon would flee, never to return. "And when you approach her, rise up, both of you, and cry out to the merciful God, and he will save you and have mercy on you" (Tobit 6:17).

And so it turned out. The marriage was arranged; the demon fled to the remotest parts of Egypt; and Tobias and Sarah prayed earnestly to God. Meanwhile, her father was out digging a grave—"with the thought, 'Perhaps he too will die'" (Tobit 8:10).

In the morning, when Tobias and Sarah were discovered very much alive, the bride's father glorified God. Then he threw a party that went on for two weeks.

After Tobias collected the money that was the original object of the expedition, Raphael advised, "Let us run ahead of your wife and prepare the house. And take the gall of the fish with you" (Tobit 11:3–4). So they left, still accompanied by the dog.

The joyous reunion was made even more joyous when Tobias restored his father's sight by rubbing the gall on his eyes. Later Sarah was welcomed into the family, and there were happy endings all around.

All that remained was for Tobias's faithful friend to be paid his promised wages. By this time Tobias had grown quite fond of "Azarias"—and with good reason, as Tobias pointed out to Tobit. "He has led me back to you safely, he cured my wife, he obtained the money for me, and he also healed you" (Tobit 12:3–4).

So Tobit offered Raphael half of the money he and Tobias had brought back. Half of an awful lot of money is still an awful lot of money, which is something angels don't have much use for. So it was time for the big revelation.

Raphael glorified God, gave his friends a little advice and then announced, "I am Raphael, one of the seven holy angels who present the prayers of the saints and enter into the presence of the glory of the Lord" (Tobit 12:15).

Naturally Tobit and Tobias were frightened at the sudden revelation of Raphael's glory, but he reassured them. "And now bless the Lord upon the earth and give thanks to God, for I am ascending to him who sent me. Write in a book everything that has happened" (Tobit 12:20).

GRACE BUILDS ON NATURE

In the story of Tobias, Raphael brought healing of soul, body and relationships. Notice that Raphael used natural means of healing, even though—as an angel on a mission from God—he could presumably have accomplished the same thing supernaturally.

This is a good lesson in how providence works. Indeed, it serves as a metaphor for the way the sacraments work. *For grace builds on nature.* Even the sacraments use material from nature—oil, wine, water, bread—to convey their supernatural grace.

And Raphael worked wonders not only with natural goods but even with natural disasters. What we would ordinarily call catastrophes—blindness, multiple widowhood, destitution, estrangement—all these became providential channels of grace by the time the threads of the story were all wound up in the end.

Raphael's many patronages are derived from incidents in the story of Tobias. Of course he's the patron of singles in search of a mate. He is the patron of pharmacists, because he provided the salve of healing. He is the patron of people who are visually impaired, because he healed Tobit's blindness; of people who are ill, because his name itself means healing; of travelers, because he went with Tobias on a dangerous journey; and of youth, because he helped young Tobias and Sarah find their destined happiness.

In art Raphael is often shown holding a flask, walking with Tobias. Sometimes one of them is carrying a fish. His liturgical memorial is September 29, along with his coarchangels.

Raphael's story remains a model for those who would enjoy the friendship of the angels. The nineteenth-century Oratorian Father Frederick Faber wrote a long poetic tribute to Raphael, with a lovely, wistful ending:

> Art thou angel, blessed Raphael!
>   Or a man in angel's guise?
> Or His likeness, who took on Him
>   Fallen man's infirmities?
> Thou wouldst long to be incarnate
>   So to share the Saviour's part;
> For the angels' spirit in thee
>   Beateth strangely like a heart![2]

Chapter Eleven

 SPIRITUAL WARFARE

> "Hear now," said he, "in regard to faith. There are
> two angels with a man—one of righteousness, and the
> other of iniquity."[1]

. . . . . .

Y*ou've seen the comic strip a hundred times. When a cartoonist wants to* show someone facing a moral dilemma, he draws a character with a little angel on one shoulder and a little devil on the other. The image goes back to at least the first century AD. That's when the *Shepherd* of Hermas was written, from which we have the above quote.

It turns out that the guardian angels aren't the only ones who take a personal interest in each one of us. Behind the scenes of Creation, history and everyday life, a battle is raging. Angels from heaven and hell fight for every soul, and one of those souls is yours. We are caught up in the battle, whether we are aware of it or not. How much better to be aware!

Hermas's heavenly interlocutor explains how to recognize the influence of the good angel:

The angel of righteousness is gentle and modest, meek and peaceful. When, therefore, he ascends into your heart, he talks to you of righteousness, purity, chastity, contentment, and of every righteous deed and glorious virtue. When all these ascend into your heart, know that the angel of righteousness is with you. These are the deeds of the angel of righteousness. Trust him, then, and his works.[2]

As you might guess, it's not hard to recognize the work of the evil angel if we put our minds to it:

"Look now at the works of the angel of iniquity. First, he is wrathful, and bitter, and foolish, and his works are evil, and ruin the servants of God. When, then, he ascends into your heart, know him by his works."

And I said to him, "How, sir, I shall perceive him, I do not know."

"Hear and understand," said he. "When anger comes upon you, or harshness, know that he is in you; and you will know this to be the case also, when you are attacked by a longing after many transactions, and the richest delicacies, and drunken revels, and various luxuries, and things improper, and by a hankering after women, and by overreaching, and pride, and blustering, and by whatever is like to these. When these ascend into your heart, know that the angel of iniquity is in you."[3]

THE BATTLE IS REAL

We might be tempted to think that this is all an elaborate metaphor—that the angels of good and evil merely represent our own good and evil tendencies struggling for mastery of our own private brains. Satan loves it when we think that way. Making people believe he doesn't exist is one of his favorite tricks. As soon as we stop believing in him, we're wide open to the subtle arguments he makes.

The earliest Christians were as keenly aware of the reality of the evil spirits as they were of the angels. Saint Paul warns us to be on our guard, not against imaginary personifications of evil tendencies but against real beings bent on evil and destruction:

> Put on the whole armor of God, that you may be able to stand against the wiles of the devil. For we are not contending against flesh and blood, but against the principalities, against the powers, against the world rulers of this present darkness, against the spiritual hosts of wickedness in the heavenly places. (Ephesians 6:11–12)

Indifference is one of Satan's two great weapons—we could call it the "while England slept" strategy. Satan can win the battle—even if not the war—when we let our guard down and pretend that there is no evil at work.

Paradoxically, Satan's other great weapon is exactly the opposite, but it works just as well. If we're so keenly aware of him that we fall into a disordered terror, that pleases Satan too. If we're so paralyzed with fear that we give up without a fight, he can just march in and take over. I call this the "shock and awe" strategy.

The healthy attitude is somewhere in the middle. There's a war going on, and it's no use pretending there isn't. But it's a war we can and will win if we stay on God's side. Remember the parable Jesus told:

> The kingdom of heaven may be compared to a man who sowed good seed in his field; but while men were sleeping, his

enemy came and sowed weeds among the wheat, and went away. So when the plants came up and bore grain, then the weeds appeared also. And the servants of the householder came and said to him, "Sir, did you not sow good seed in your field? How then has it weeds?" He said to them, "An enemy has done this." The servants said to him, "Then do you want us to go and gather them?" But he said, "No; lest in gathering the weeds you root up the wheat along with them. Let both grow together until the harvest; and at harvest time I will tell the reapers, Gather the weeds first and bind them in bundles to be burned, but gather the wheat into my barn." (Matthew 13:24–30)

HOW SATAN WORKS

If you want a first-rate primer on how the powers of evil work, you don't need to look any further than the temptations of Christ. Satan pulled out all the stops there, but he used the same wicked strategies with Christ that he tries against us every day.

We can find the best-known version of the story at the beginning of the fourth chapter of Matthew. After his Baptism Jesus was led into the desert by the Spirit, and there Satan offered him three temptations.

The first: "If you are the Son of God, command these stones to become loaves of bread." And Jesus answered, "It is written, 'Man shall not live by bread alone, but by every word that proceeds from the mouth of God'" (Matthew 4:3–4).

Here Satan offered a straightforward temptation. "You're hungry," he said. "Prove you're the Son of God. Do something spectacular and make the hunger go away." Jesus' answer was straightforward too: He quoted Scripture to remind Satan that there are more important things than hunger.

So Satan came up with another idea.

> Then the devil took him to the holy city, and set him on the pinnacle of the temple, and said to him, "If you are the Son of God, throw yourself down; for it is written,
>
> 'He will give his angels charge of you,'
> and
>
> 'On their hands they will bear you up, lest you strike your foot against a stone.'"
>
> Jesus said to him, "Again it is written, 'You shall not tempt the Lord your God.'" (Matthew 4:5–7)

Satan can rattle off Bible verses just as easily as Jesus can. God wouldn't let anything bad happen to you, right? Prove it.

This is a temptation Satan offers us over and over: *If there really is a good God*, he whispers in our ear, *surely he wouldn't let bad things happen to good people. And if bad things do happen to good people, that means…*

But Jesus reminded Satan of what we all need to remember: Putting God to the test is denying faith. Here is a perfect example of what we said earlier about the guardian angels. When we see things from their perspective, we realize that *physical* harm isn't as dangerous as spiritual death through sin.

Finally Satan offered the most insidious temptation of all:

> Again, the devil took him to a very high mountain, and showed him all the kingdoms of the world and the glory of them; and he said to him, "All these I will give you, if you will fall down and worship me."

Then Jesus said to him, "Begone, Satan! for it is written,

'You shall worship the Lord your God

and him only shall you serve.'" (Matthew 4:8–10)

All the power in the world! That's a pretty good offer. After all, Jesus came to save humanity. Think of the good he could do if he controlled the government of every nation!

Satan is offering us this same deal all the time. Perhaps the terms aren't quite so generous for most of us, but the basic form is the same: You can do a lot of good if only you'll compromise a bit on your principles.

We only need to open the door a little bit for Satan to get his foot in. And that's really all he needs. Let him get his foot in the door, and he can take over the whole house.

POSSESSION

There are indications that demonic possessions have been increasing in recent years. In 2002 London's *The Spectator* reported on a seeming epidemic in the Tuscany region in Italy. A German priest, Father Joerg Mueller, told the *London Times* that in 2007 alone he received requests for exorcism from "around 350 people who think they are possessed by an evil spirit.... Therapy hasn't worked for them; they want exorcism—a prayer that can free them." Rome's chief exorcist, Father Gabriele Amorth, told *The Telegraph* that he has performed the ritual tens of thousands of times throughout his decades of ministry. And in 2008 *The Washington Post* noted the Polish Church's establishment of a large center dedicated entirely to doing exorcisms.[4]

Yet possession probably represents a relatively small portion of the devil's activity on earth—a dramatic portion, yes, and intended to strike fear in our hearts. But possession is most effective (I believe) as a distraction. If the devil can persuade us to fear his "power" and doubt God's protection, he can occupy our minds endlessly with needless and useless worry. And while we're cowering before his "shock and awe" tactics, we're neglecting the drab, ordinary temptations we face at home and at work. We give in to laziness, impatience, rudeness, lying and passive lust. And then the enemy has his foot in the door.

Most of the time the devil doesn't need to take extraordinary measures to get us to do his bidding. Why should he mount an invasion when he can get people to willingly be his vassals, pay him tribute and do as he wishes?

If we want to keep the devil at a distance, we should—in the words of Tradition—avoid any near occasions of sin.

Still, possession does happen, and we should never give in to the fashionable skepticism that dismisses it as medieval sorcery. The stories are there in the Gospels: Casting out demons was one of the things that made Jesus' reputation as a miracle worker. The same kinds of possession still happen today. We read about them occasionally in newspapers and magazines.

How does possession happen? It seems often to be sort of like burglary. If we leave the door open, the crooks walk right in. When we deal with the occult, the world of black magic or other areas of evil, then we leave the door wide open. According to a second-century North African writer, the devil once complained to an exorcist that he had every right to take possession of a certain woman. She, after all, had been attending salacious shows in the theatre. "I did it all most righteously," the devil said (with a smirk, I'm sure), "for I found her in my domain."[5]

In the real-life story on which the movie *The Exorcist* was based, the victim, as an adolescent boy, had been using a Ouija board trying to contact spirits. He made contact all right, and the spirits held control of him for years. His journey to deliverance was humbling and served as his introduction to the Catholic faith.

He had been raised Protestant, but his pastors were powerless against the demon and urged him to contact a Catholic priest. It took years and many failed attempts before a successful expulsion took place—and according to the victim, that happened only because Saint Michael the archangel intervened.

So here's a simple piece of advice: Don't dabble in the occult. Don't go to fortune-tellers. Don't play with Ouija boards. Fight your battles far from the city walls. Avoid occasions of sin.

You are a child of God. You commune with the Almighty, and his angels are at your disposal. The saints are around you like a great cloud of witness (see Hebrews 12:1). You don't need the frisson of demonic tricks. It's not worth the consequences.

DEMON REPELLANTS

If you do sense the presence of Satan or evil spirits—even if it's just that cartoon devil on your shoulder whispering in your ear— then get help. And help is available.

Satan recoils from anything holy. Saint Athanasius said that "by the sign of the cross...all magic is stayed, all sorcery confounded, all the idols are abandoned."[6]

There's a hint of truth in those old vampire movies. The devil recoils at the name of Jesus. Holy water, crucifixes and other overt signs of faith repel him. The great mystic of the Counter-Reformation, Saint Teresa of Avila, put holy water to good use. She "learned from experience that there is nothing that chases devils away for good like holy water."7 And she recounts, in detail, several of her own "victories by water."

Frequent reception of the sacrament of Holy Communion can keep us fortified and well-armed against any attacks. Says Saint John Chrysostom: "Let us, then, come back from that table like lions breathing out fire, thus becoming terrifying to the Devil, and remaining mindful of our Head and of the love he has shown for us." And a little later he adds: "This Blood, when worthily received, drives away demons and puts them at a distance from us, and even summons to us angels and the Lord of angels."8 Going to Mass repels Satan, and there's usually no reason you can't do it several times a week.

Whatever is holy repels Satan. Reading the Bible with a faithful heart and a willingness to learn from it repels him. Earnest prayer repels him—even if it's only the childish rhyming prayers you remember from when you were young. Spending time with a good spiritual book—a book about the angels, perhaps —may help you conquer Satan's temptations and give you the strength you need to resist him. Frequent confession is another great inoculator against the works of Satan.

Perhaps the best weapons against the evil angels, however, are the good angels. We can call on our guardian angels to help us in times of temptation. The good angels always win—if we give them half a chance.

 THE ANGELS AND US

. . . .

Iƒ *we're not thinking with the angels, and consciously, we're just skimming* the surface of Christianity; we're not thinking biblically. The Wisdom of Solomon tells us that knowledge of angels is the mark of a righteous man:

> When a righteous man [Jacob] fled from his brother's wrath,
> she [Wisdom] guided him on straight paths;
> she showed him the kingdom of God,
> and gave him knowledge of angels; she prospered him in his
>   labors,
> and increased the fruit of his toil. (Wisdom 10:10)

We're no different from Jacob and our other ancestors in faith. We walk in the company of angels. We hope to live in their company forever. That makes—or at least it should make—a fundamental difference in how we live.

THE TROUBLE WITH ANGELS: THE DANGER OF IDOLATRY
After all this talk about the power of angels and how much good they can do us, we ought to have a pretty high opinion of them. And that's perfectly justified. Angels are great and powerful beings.

But they are not gods. There is only one God, and we must not forget that.

"See to it that no one makes a prey of you by philosophy and empty deceit, according to human tradition, according to the elemental spirits of the universe, and not according to Christ," Paul warned the Colossians. "Let no one disqualify you, insisting on self-abasement and worship of angels, taking his stand on visions, puffed up without reason by his sensuous mind" (Colossians 2:8, 18).

The angels themselves—the good angels, that is—make the same distinction. Remember what happened when Saint John tried to worship an angel: "I fell down at his feet to worship him, but he said to me, 'You must not do that! I am a fellow servant with you and your brethren who hold the testimony of Jesus. Worship God'" (Revelation 19:10).

The worship of angels can be a genuine danger. The ancient rabbis recognized it as one of the causes of idolatry. Here's a story from the Babylonian Talmud:

> R. Isaac opened (his discourse) with the text: *"The Lord is my portion," said my soul; therefore will I hope in Him* (Lam. 3:24). R. Isaac said: "This may be compared to a king who entered a province with his generals, rulers and governors. Some of the citizens of the province chose a general as their patron, others a ruler and others a governor. One of them who was cleverer than the rest, said, "I will choose the king." Why? All others are liable to change, but the king is never changed. Likewise, when God came down to Sinai, there also came down with Him many companies of angels (Num. 2:3). Michael and his company, Gabriel and his company. Some of

> the nations of the world chose for themselves (as their
> patron) Michael, others Gabriel, but Israel chose God for
> itself, exclaiming, "The Lord is my portion," said my soul.
> This is the force of "Hear, O Israel, the Lord, our God, the
> Lord is One."[1]

When Jesus revealed the new law, it didn't take long for the old temptations to reassert themselves among the Christians. Even while the apostles were still alive, sects grew up that claimed to have secret knowledge of angels and incomprehensible things. The Gnostics—with their angelic emanations and aeons and archons and secret passwords—grew into a real danger to orthodox Christianity.

In many ways this was the old paganism dressed up in new clothes. Indeed, the early Christians thoroughly believed that the pagan gods were nothing more than demons—evil angels—who had taken advantage of the natural human tendency to worship such powerful spirits.

> Those who abandoned God's service,... being enemies of the
> truth and in collusion against God, try to secure divine wor-
> ship for themselves, together with the title of gods, not
> because they want any honor—what honor could they have in
> their abandoned state?—nor to hurt God, who cannot be
> hurt, but to hurt man: it is man they are striving so hard to
> divert from knowledge and worship of the true greatness, in
> case man gains the immortality which they have lost by their
> own wickedness.[2]

Nothing terrified these demons more than the gospel—the message that Christ is truly the Son of God, come to undo the works of the devil. Saint Paulinus of Nola, who grew up in what is now Bordeaux in late Roman times, imagined their terror in vivid language: "The neglected images in the empty temples tremble when struck by the pious voices, and are overthrown by the name of Christ. Terrified demons abandon their deserted shrines. The envious Serpent pale with rages struggles in vain, his lips blood-stained, bemoaning with this hungry throat the redemption of man."[3]

GIVING THE ANGELS THEIR DUE

Still, we must be careful not to throw the baby out with the baptismal water. An excessive fear of falling into idolatry can paralyze us, rendering us unable to love God's creatures very well at all and, oddly enough, causing us to give the devil more than his due.

Art historian Émile Mâle points out the "diabolical irony" of the actions of the Calvinist iconoclasts, who destroyed images of the angels in order to protect Christians from the danger of idolatry: "In a reredos devoted to Saint Michael, the archangel had been destroyed while the demon at his feet was spared."[4]

We can do the same when we marginalize devotion to the angels. It is good and right to remember that the Lord our God is one. But it is also good to remember the powerful beings he sends to help us. We do not worship them, but we do call on them for help—just as we might call on anyone who is stronger than we are.

The angels worship *with us*; they do their best to keep us on the straight and narrow path; they teach us and protect us.

Knowing the angels is part of being a Christian. We can't ignore them without ignoring a huge and important part of our faith.

We are also called to be angels in a sense. "Angel," after all, is the job description, not the nature of the being. An angel in the primary sense is a bearer of God's messages. It is our duty—and it ought to be our joy—to bring God's Word with us everywhere we go.

"Each one of you," said Gregory the Great, "in so far as he can, in so far as he receives an inspiration from on high—if he recalls his neighbor from his wickedness, takes care to encourage him to do good, proclaims the eternal kingdom or eternal punishment to one astray—when he provides the words of the holy message—each one of you is truly an angel."[5]

That doesn't mean we have to carry placards or grab people by the lapels and force them to listen to our sermons. Those aren't very effective techniques, and real angels tend to act more subtly anyway.

Telling people about the joy we experience in the Church is always a good thing. But what is even more effective is living a Christian life. The early Christian philosopher Tertullian saw that the Christian life was what astonished the pagans most. "'See how they love one another,' they say—for they themselves hate each other—'and how they are ready to die for each other'—for they themselves would be more ready to kill each other."[6]

Consciously imitating the angels will keep us looking like Christians. The angels have free will too, but they conform their wills completely to God's will. We should always be striving to do the same.

When we pray, "Thy will be done, on earth as it is in heaven," we should be thinking of the angels. We should be praying that we might do God's will as quickly and as unquestioningly as the angels in the heavenly court do.

We should always be hospitable to angels—and for their sake, we should be hospitable to everyone. The Good Book says: "Do not neglect to show hospitality to strangers, for thereby some have entertained angels unawares" (Hebrews 13:2). We are no better than Tobias: We may not recognize the hour of our visitation. And the angels who visit us just might dress themselves up in distressing disguises—maybe as the coworker or parish council member who opposes our dearest plans, maybe as the police officer writing a ticket.

Whenever you're particularly annoyed, stop and think about "entertaining angels unawares." Better just to assume you're dealing with an angel. That's a quick way to improve your disposition anyway, and you'll probably be happier even if you're wrong. And imagine how much better off you'll be if you're right!

Mastery of the passions is another thing we can imitate from the angels. They are not swayed by passing desires or lingering anger. And in the heavenly kingdom, we too will be free from all the passions that distract us from God's will. If we can learn to exercise that freedom now, we'll be that much closer to heaven.

But it's hard to imitate angels, isn't it? After all, we're only human. We have bodies that subject us to overwhelming temptations every time we see a piece of chocolate we shouldn't eat. How could we possibly hope to be anything like the angels?

We can ask the angels to help us, train us, push us and carry us when we're feeling particularly weak.

Heavenly Helpers

When our lives are troubled by mice in the walls or poison ivy in the backyard, we know what measures to take. But when we're troubled by moral temptations, painful memories or an anxious imagination, it's sometimes a little trickier to figure out what to do. Human means and medical means sometimes help. But intellectual and psychological difficulties often have spiritual and moral dimensions too, and these are the special province of the angels.

Maybe you're troubled by memories of sin, and this leads you to worry over God's forgiveness. Maybe you worry whether the memory itself is an occasion of sin. Some people are bothered by regret, and they keep going over their past failures to love their parents, children or friends.

If this is your particular difficulty, ask your guardian angel to stand as a sentry at the gates of your memory. He can do it. The angels can exercise a tremendous influence over our intellect, will and other faculties. So ask, and ask again, and ask again. Our angels can help us let go and give our unchangeable past over to God, who heals all wounds—even, ultimately, the wounds of the dead.

But maybe the past isn't your problem; maybe you're bothered by anxieties about the future, your imagination conjuring up an infinite variety of catastrophic scenarios. This too is a job for the angels. Ask yours to stand guard over your imagination. Ask him to stay as a gatekeeper of your imagination, as the cherubim were gatekeepers at Eden (see Genesis 3:24).

We should not despise popular devotion, even—perhaps especially—when it seems most childlike. The "Angel of God" prayer is simple and easy to remember, and it expresses perfectly what we need to say. The ever-popular Hail Mary begins with an angel's greeting; we should make it our own. As we've seen, the Mass is charged with the grandeur of angelic prayers. And even the Our Father can be interpreted as a plea for a more angelic life—"on earth as it is in heaven."

If we simply stick to the basics, but with renewed attention, we'll stay close to the good angels, which will lead us ever closer to the good God.

And in the end that's where we want to be.

. . . . .

So here we are at the back of the book. We've looked at how the Bible describes angels, what the early Christians believed about them and what the Church believes about them today. Now what?

If there's one thing I want every reader to take away from this book, it's a sense of the constant presence of the angels. We should keep the angels in our minds all the time, because they can be a great help to us when we need them.

So here, at the back of the book where they're easy to find, are some things to keep the angels in our minds and close to our hearts—some prayers, poems and hymns that have helped many people feel closer to the angels.

 PRAYERS

THE ANGELUS (prayed at noon)

V/. The angel of the Lord declared unto Mary, R/. And she conceived by the Holy Spirit.

Hail Mary, full of grace, the Lord is with thee (Luke 1:28).

Blessed art thou among women,

and blessed is the fruit of thy womb, Jesus (Luke 1:42). Holy Mary, Mother of God,

pray for us sinners, now and at the hour of our death. Amen.

V/. "Behold the handmaid of the Lord." R/. "Be it done unto me according to thy word."

Hail Mary, full of grace …

V/. And the Word was made flesh, R/. And dwelt among us.

Hail Mary, full of grace …

V/. Pray for us, O Holy Mother of God. R/. That we may be made worthy of the promises of Christ.

Let us pray: Pour forth, we beseech thee, O Lord,

thy grace into our hearts,

that we to whom the incarnation of Christ thy Son

was made known by the message of an angel,

may by his passion and cross be brought to the glory of his resurrection;

through the same Christ our Lord. Amen.

THE GUARDIAN ANGEL PRAYER

Angel of God, my guardian dear,

to whom God's love commits me here,

ever this day be at my side

to light and guard, to rule and guide. Amen.

AN ANGEL PRAYER FOR THE HOME

O Lord, we ask you to visit this home
and drive from it all the snares of the enemy.
Let your holy angels dwell here, to preserve us in peace;
and may your blessing be upon us forever,
through our Lord Jesus Christ. Amen.[1]

ANOTHER GUARDIAN ANGEL PRAYER

O most faithful companion, appointed by God to be my guide
    and protector:
you are ever at my side.
What thanks can I offer you for your faithfulness and love
and for all the benefits which you have conferred upon me?
You watch over me in sleep;
you console me when I am sad;
you lift me up when I fall;
you avert the dangers that threaten me;
you prepare me for the future;
you withdraw me from evil and encourage me to good;
you exhort me to penance when I yield to temptation
and reconcile me to my offended God.

Long since should I have been cast into hell,
but by your prayers you averted from me the anger of God.
Do not leave me, then, I beg you;
but still comfort me in adversity,
restrain me in prosperity,
defend me in danger,
assist me in temptations, lest at any time I fall a victim to them.

Offer to God my prayers and groanings and all my religious
exercises,

and obtain for me the great gift of final perseverance,

and the grace to die in the friendship of my Creator,

and so to enter into life everlasting. Amen.[2]

The Saint Michael Prayer

· By Pope Leo XIII ·

Saint Michael the Archangel, defend us in battle.

Be our protection against the wickedness and snares
of the devil;

May God rebuke him, we humbly pray.

And do thou, O prince of the heavenly host,

by the power of God,

cast into hell Satan and all evil spirits

who prowl through the world seeking the ruin of
souls.

Amen.

A Longer Saint Michael Prayer

*In 1890 Pope Leo XIII approved a much longer prayer to Saint Michael. In 1902
that prayer was in turn replaced by a mid-sized version, which follows.*

Most glorious prince of the heavenly armies, Saint Michael the
archangel,

defend us in our battle against principalities and powers,

against the rulers of this world of darkness,

against the spirits of wickedness in the high places (Ephesians
6:12).

Come to the assistance of men whom God has created to his
likeness

and whom he has redeemed at a great price from the tyranny of
the devil.

Holy Church venerates you as her guardian and protector;

to you the Lord has entrusted the souls of the redeemed to be led into heaven.

Pray therefore the God of peace to crush Satan beneath our feet,

that he may no longer retain men captive and do injury to the Church.

Offer our prayers to the Most High,

that without delay they may draw his mercy down upon us;

take hold of "the dragon, the old serpent, which is the devil and Satan,"

bind him and cast him into the bottomless pit

"so that he may no longer seduce the nations" (Revelation 20:2).[3]

PRAYER FOR THE DEAD

O Lord Jesus Christ, glorious king, spare the souls of the faithful departed

from the pains of hell and from the deep pit; free them from the jaws of the lion,

and let them not descend into hell to be swallowed up in darkness. May Saint Michael, your standard bearer, lead them into the holy light which you promised of old to Abraham and his posterity. O Lord Jesus Christ, King of glory,

deliver the souls of all the faithful departed from the pains of hell and from the deep pit:

deliver them from the mouth of the lion, that hell may not swallow them up,

and they may not fall into darkness;

but may the holy standard-bearer Michael

introduce them to the holy light,

which you promised of old to Abraham and his seed.[4]

Prayer to Saint Raphael for Happy Meetings
Attributed to Ernest Hello, 1964.

O Raphael, lead us toward those we are waiting for, those who
are waiting for us: Raphael, angel of happy meeting, lead us
by the hand toward those we are looking for. May all our
movements be guided by your light and transfigured with
your joy.

Angel, guide of Tobias, lay the request we now address to you
at the feet of him on whose unveiled face you are privileged
to gaze.

Lonely and tired, crushed by the separations and sorrows of life,
we feel the need of calling you and of pleading for the protection
  of your wings,

so that we may not be as strangers in the province of joy,

all ignorant of the concerns of our country.

Remember the weak, you who are strong,

you whose home lies beyond the region of thunder,

in a land that is always peaceful,

always serene and bright with the resplendent glory of God.[5]

Based on the Mass Prayers for the
Feast of Saint Raphael

O God,

You gave blessed Raphael the archangel

to your servant Tobias for a companion on the way;

grant that we your servants may ever be protected by his
  guardianship

and strengthened by his help.

The angel of the Lord, Raphael, took and bound the devil.

Great is our Lord, and great is his power. Alleluia, alleluia.

I will sing praise to you in the sight of the angels;

I will worship toward your holy temple, and I will give glory to your name, O Lord. Alleluia.

Direct, O Lord God, the holy archangel Raphael to our help;

and may he, whom we believe to be ever in attendance on Your Majesty,

present our poor petitions to you for your blessing.[6]

HEALING PRAYER: TO SAINT RAPHAEL

Glorious archangel Saint Raphael, great prince of the heavenly court, you are illustrious for your gifts of wisdom and grace. You are a guide of those who journey by land or sea or air, consoler of the afflicted, and refuge of sinners.

I beg you, assist me in all my needs and in all the sufferings of this life, as once you helped the young Tobias on his travels. Because you are the "medicine of God" I humbly pray you to heal the many infirmities of my soul and the ills that afflict my body. I especially ask of you the favor (here mention your special intention) and the great grace of purity to prepare me to be the temple of the Holy Spirit. Amen.[7]

Prayer to Saint Gabriel for Strength

Blessed Saint Gabriel, archangel,

we beseech you to intercede for us at the throne of divine mercy:

As you announced the mystery of the Incarnation to Mary,

so through your prayers may we receive strength of faith and
courage of spirit,

and thus find favor with God and redemption through Christ
Our Lord.

May we sing the praise of God our Savior with the angels and
saints

in heaven forever and ever. Amen.[8]

Based on the Mass Prayers for the Feast of Saint Gabriel

O God, from amidst the angels you chose the archangel Gabriel
to announce the mystery of your incarnation;

mercifully grant that we who celebrate his feast upon earth
may enjoy his patronage in heaven.

May the offering of our service and the prayer of the blessed
archangel Gabriel

be accepted in your sight, O Lord;

so that, as he is venerated by us on earth,

so may he be our advocate with you in heaven.[9]

In Paradisum (Prayer for the Dead)

Come to his [her] assistance, you saints of God;

meet him [her], O angels of the Lord.

Receive his [her] soul, and present it in the sight of the Most
High.

May Christ, who called you, receive you;

and may the angels lead you into the bosom of Abraham.

Receive his [her] soul and present it in the sight of the Most
High.[10]

 Poems

Guardian Angel
By John Henry Newman

My oldest friend, mine from the hour
   When first I drew my breath;
My faithful friend, that shall be mine,
   Unfailing, till my death;

Thou hast been ever at my side;
   My Maker to thy trust
Consign'd my soul, what time He framed
   The infant child of dust.

No beating heart in holy prayer,
   No faith, inform'd aright,
Gave me to Joseph's tutelage,
   Or Michael's conquering might.

Nor patron Saint, nor Mary's love,
   The dearest and the best,
Has known my being, as thou hast known,
   And blest, as thou hast blest,

Thou wast my sponsor at the font;
   And thou, each budding year,
Didst whisper elements of truth
   Into my childish ear.

And when, ere boyhood yet was gone,
   My rebel spirit fell,

Ah! thou didst see, and shudder too,
　　Yet bear each deed of Hell.

And then in turn, when judgments came,
　　And scared me back again,
Thy quick soft breath was near to soothe
　　And hallow every pain.

Oh! who of all thy toils and cares
　　Can tell the tale complete,
To place me under Mary's smile
　　And Peter's royal feet!

And thou wilt hang about my bed,
　　When life is ebbing low;
Of doubt, impatience, and of gloom,
　　The jealous sleepless foe.

Mine, when I stand before the Judge;
　　And mine, if spared to stay
Within the golden furnace, till
　　My sin is burn'd away.

And mine, O Brother of my soul,
　　When my release shall come;
Thy gentle arms shall lift me then,
　　Thy wings shall waft me home.[11]

Saint Michael the Weigher

By James Russell Lowell

Stood the tall Archangel weighing
All man's dreaming, doing, saying,
All the failure and the pain,
All the triumph and the gain,
In the unimagined years,
Full of hopes, more full of tears,
Since old Adam's hopeless eyes
Backward searched for Paradise,
And, instead, the flame-blade saw
Of inexorable Law.

Waking, I beheld him there,
With his fire-gold, flickering hair,
In his blinding armor stand,
And the scales were in his hand:
Mighty were they, and full well
They could poise both heaven and hell.
"Angel," asked I humbly then,
"Weighest thou the souls of men?
That thine office is, I know."
"Nay," he answered me, "not so;
But I weigh the hope of Man
Since the power of choice began,
In the world, of good or ill."
Then I waited and was still.

In one scale I saw him place
All the glories of our race,
Cups that lit Belshazzar's feast,

Gems, the lightning of the East,
Kublai's sceptre, Cæsar's sword,
Many a poet's golden word,
Many a skill of science, vain
To make men as gods again.

In the other scale he threw
Things regardless, outcast, few,
Martyr-ash, arena sand,
Of Saint Francis' cord a strand,
Beechen cups of men whose need
Fasted that the poor might feed,
Disillusions and despairs
Of young saints with grief-grayed hairs,
Broken hearts that brake for Man.

Marvel through my pulses ran,
Seeing then the beam divine
Swiftly on this hand decline,
While Earth's splendor and renown
Mounted light as thistle-down.[12]

 HYMNS

O HOLY ANGEL
(To the tune of "The King of Love My Savior Is")

O holy Angel, Guardian mine,
My guide and my director,
Sweet messenger of love divine,
Be thou my kind protector.

By day or night whate'er betide,
Oh, fold thy wings around me:
And never, never leave my side
In dangers that surround me.

O, bear to God my fervent pray'r,
Preserve me from temptation!
Extend thy help, thy loving care,
To work out my salvation.

While here a pilgrim weak and frail,
Blest Angel walk before me;
And when my strength begins to fail,
Oh, kindly then restore me.

Be near me, Angel, when I die,
Till over sin victorious,
Thou bear my parting soul on high
To reign with Jesus glorious.[13]

SWEET ANGEL OF MERCY
By M. Caswell

Sweet angel of mercy,
By heaven's decree,
Benignly appointed
To watch over me.
Without thy protection
So constant and nigh,
I could not well live,
I should perish and die.

All thanks for thy love,
Dear companion and friend!
Oh! may it continue
With me to the end.
Oh! cease not to keep me,
Blest guide of my youth,
In th'way of religion,
And virtue and truth.

Support me in weakness,
My spirit inflame;
Defend me in danger,
Secure me from shame,
That safe from temptation
And sudden surprise,
I may mount the straight path
That ascends to the skies.

When I wander in error,
My footsteps recall;

Remove from my pathway
What causes my fall;
Preserve me from sin,
And in all that I do
May God and His glory
Be ever in view.[14]

MY ANGEL AND DEFENDER

Translated from Latin by D. J. Donahoe

My Angel and Defender,
   In love I call to thee,
The Guide and gentle Teacher
   That Heaven has sent to me.
Thanks for thy loving kindness
   My soul desires to give;
I would not die without thee
   Nor would I dare to live.

O Master kind and Comrade,
   Direct my wavering will,
Be near me as my Leader,
   Be my Defender still,
And keep me in the pathway
   That leads to fields above;
Enkindle in my bosom
   The fire of sacred love.

When I am sad bring comfort,
   When weak thy power display,
In thy dear arms upbear me

Across each rugged way.
Let not my footsteps falter
   Along the road of right,
Make safe for me the journey
   Of justice and of light.

My Comrade thou since childhood,
   In truth and love sincere,
O fail me not, sweet Angel,
   When death's dark hour is near.
Then aid my will to conquer
   The malice of the foe;
What most to God is pleasing
   To my faint spirit show.

And in my final struggle
   A true contrition bring,
That after pure confession
   No stains of earth may cling.
In piety and patience,
   In faith and hope and love,
So I may leave the regions
   Of earth for life above.

And when my trembling spirit
   Before the Judge shall stand,
Bring then thy aid, dear Angel,
   Be thou at my right hand..
O loving Guide and Comrade,
   In all my wandering way;
Be always near to lead me
   To Heaven's eternal Day.[15]

Acknowledgments
1. Coventry Patmore, "Going to Church," *The Angel in the House* (London: Cassell, 1891), e-text at Project Gutenberg, available at: www.gutenberg.org.

Introduction: The Everywhere of Angels
1. *Roman Missal*, Preface I for Weekdays.
2. *Roman Missal*, Eucharistic Prayer I.

Chapter One: What Is an Angel?
1. Augustine, *Sermons*, Sermon 7, no. 3 (*Patrologia Latina*, 38.64), author's translation.
2. See, for example, Justin's *Dialogue With Trypho*, chaps. 76, 126, in Philip Schaff, *Ante-Nicene Fathers*, vol. 1, pp. 236, 262, available at: www.ccel.org.
3. Justin Martyr, *Dialogue With Trypho*, chap. 58, in Schaff, vol. 1, p. 226.
4. Gregory the Great, *Moralia in Job*, vol. 1, bk. 6, no. 20. All passages quoted from the *Moralia* are adapted from the translation of John Henry Parker, *Morals on the Book of Job*, www.lectionarycentral.com.
5. Adapted from Gregory the Great, *Moralia in Job*, vol. 1, bk. 2, no. 3.

Chapter Two: The Testing of Angels
1. Albert S. Cook, ed., *Milton's Paradise Lost* (Boston: Leach, Shewell, & Sanborn, 1806), p. 54.
2. Adapted from Gregory the Great, *Moralia in Job*, vol. 1, bk. 5, no. 68.
3. *Milton's Paradise Lost*, p. 62.
4. Adapted from Gregory the Great, *Moralia in Job*, vol. 1, bk. 4, no. 8.

Chapter Three: Angels in the Old Testament
1. Gregory the Great, *Forty Gospel Homilies*, Dom David Hurst, trans. (Kalamazoo, Mich.: Cistercian, 1990), p. 285.

Chapter Four: Angels in the New Testament
1. Gregory the Great, *Gospel Homilies*, 8, 2, quoted in Josemaría Escrivá, *Christ Is Passing By: Homilies* (Princeton, N.J.: Scepter, 1974), p. 438.
2. Ignatius of Loyola, *Letters of St. Ignatius of Loyola*, William J. Young, ed. (Chicago: Loyola, 1959), p. 125.

Chapter Five: The Kinds of Angels

1. Gregory the Great, *Gospel Homilies*, 34, quoted in "Angel," *The Catholic Encyclopedia* (New York: Robert Appleton, 1907), volume 1, p. 478.

2. Adapted from Gregory the Great, *Moralia in Job*, vol. 1, bk. 4, no. 55, www.lectionarycentral.com.

3. Denis, *The Celestial Hierarchy*, vol. 2, p. 113, quoted in Mike Aquilina, *The Fathers of the Church: Expanded Edition* (Huntington, Ind.: Our Sunday Visitor, 2006), p. 237.

4. Denis, in Aquilina, pp. 237–239.

Chapter Six: Guardian Angels

1. Jerome, *Commentary on Matthew*, quoted in "Guardian Angel," *The Catholic Encyclopedia* (New York: The Encyclopedia Press, 1912), vol. 7, p. 49.

2. Quoted in Helen T. Verongos and Alan Cowell, "Muriel Spark, Novelist Who Wrote 'The Prime of Miss Jean Brodie,' Dies at 88," *New York Times*, April 16, 2006, www.nytimes.com.

3. Phil Taylor, "Color barriers don't fall easy, but they fall," *Pittsburgh Catholic*, November 3, 1995, p. 5.

4. Francis Fernandez-Carvajal, *In Conversation with God: Meditations for each day of the year*, vol. 7, *Feasts: July–December* (London: Scepter, 2005), p. 186.

5. Flannery O'Connor, *The Habit of Being: Letters of Flannery O'Connor* (New York: Vintage, 1980), pp. 131–132.

6. Origen, quoted in Jean Danielou, *The Angels and Their Mission: According to the Fathers of the Church*, David Heimann, trans. (Notre Dame, Ind.: Ave Maria, 1987), p. 58.

7. Adapted from Gregory the Great, *Moralia in Job*, vol. 1, bk. 17, no. 17, www.lectionarycentral.com.

8. Josemaría Escrivá, *The Way* (Manila: Sinag-Tala, 1982), p. 190.

Chapter Seven: The Angels at Worship

1. John Chrysostom, "Homily on the Ascension of Our Lord Jesus Christ," *Patrologia Graeca*, 50.441a, author's translation, emphasis added.

2. Scott Hahn, "The Cathedral: Where Heaven and Earth Meet," *A Reflection of Faith: Saint Paul Cathedral, Pittsburgh 1906–2006* (Pittsburgh: Saint Paul Cathedral Parish, 2007), pp. 15–16.

3. Socrates Scholasticus, *Ecclesiastical History*, bk. 6, chap. 8, adapted from the translation in Philip Schaff and Henry Wace, eds., *Nicene and Post-Nicene Fathers*, vol. 2, *Socrates, Sozomenus: Church Histories*, p. 144.

4. Quoted in Jean Danielou, *The Bible and the Liturgy* (Notre Dame, Ind.: University of Notre Dame Press, 1956), p. 135.

5. John Chrysostom, *On Priesthood*, 6.4, adapted from the translation in *Nicene and Post-Nicene Fathers*, vol. 9, p. 76.

6. From a midrash on Psalm 78, quoted in Edward J. Kilmartin, *The Eucharist in the Primitive Church* (Englewood Cliffs, N.J.: Prentice-Hall, 1965), p. 14.

7. Eucharistic Prayer I, *Roman Missal.*

Chapter Eight: Michael, Our Defender

1. Jacobus de Voragine, compiler, *The Golden Legend*, vol. 5, William Caxton, trans., from F. S. Ellis, ed., *Temple Classics* (Edinburgh: Constable, 1900). I have modernized the language from Caxton's translation. Available at: www.fordham.edu.

2. Gregory the Great, *Gospel Homilies*, 34, *Patrologia Latina*, 76:1251A, author's translation.

Chapter Nine: Gabriel, the Great Communicator

1. Gregory the Great, *Gospel Homilies*, 34, 76:1250D, author's translation.

Chapter Ten: Raphael, Friend and Guide

1. Gregory the Great, *Gospel Homilies*, 34, 76:1251C, author's translation.

2. Frederick William Faber, "St. Raphael," in *Hymns* (London: Thomas Richardson, 1871), p. 201.

Chapter Eleven: Spiritual Warfare

1. Hermas, *The Shepherd*, bk. 2, commandment 6, chap. 2, adapted from the translation in *Ante-Nicene Fathers*, vol. 2, p. 24.

2. Hermas.

3. Hermas.

4. See Rod Williams, "Hell to Pay," *The Spectator*, January 5, 2002, cover story; Gyles Brandreth, "The Devil Is Gaining Ground," *The Telegraph*, March 11, 2000; Roger Boyes, "Exorcists Are Summoned from Abroad to Drive the Demons Away," *London Times*, May 22, 2008; Craig Whitlock, "Ritual of Dealing With Demons Undergoes a Revival," *The Washington Post*, February 11, 2008, sect. A, p. 9.

5. Tertullian tells the story in *De Spectaculis*, no. 26, author's translation.

6. Athanasius, *On the Incarnation* (Crestwood, N.Y.: St. Vladimir's Seminary Press, 1998), p. 62.

7. Teresa of Avila, *Autobiography*, chap. 31, excerpted in Jon Cowans, ed., *Early Modern Spain: A Documentary History* (Philadelphia: University of Pennsylvania Press, 2003), pp. 98–99.

8. John Chrysostom, Homily 46, *Commentary on Saint John the Apostle and Evangelist* (New York: Fathers of the Church, 1957), pp. 469, 471–472, available at: www.catholicculture.org.

Chapter Twelve: The Angels and Us

1. *Babylonian Talmud, Deuteronomy Rabbah* 2:34, quoted in Alan F. Segal, *Two Powers in Heaven: Early Rabbinic Reports about Christianity and Gnosticism* (Boston: Brill, 2002), pp. 137–138.
2. Lactantius, *The Divine Institutes*, Anthony Bowen and Peter Garnsey, trans. (Liverpool: Liverpool University Press, 2003), p. 163.
3. Paulinus of Nola, *Poem* 19.53–75, quoted in Michael Maas, *Readings in Late Antiquity: A Sourcebook* (London: Routledge, 2000), p. 32.
4. Émile Mâle, *Religious Art from the Twelfth to the Eighteenth Century* (New York: Pantheon, 1949), p. 167.
5. Gregory the Great, *Forty Gospel Homilies*, p. 32.
6. Tertullian, *Apologeticus* 39.7, author's translation.

The Back of the Book

1. Adapted from Night Prayer, available at: www.catholic-forum.com.
2. Adapted from "Prayer to Our Guardian Angel," Andrew Porro, compiler, *Manual of Prayers for the Oblates of St. Joseph* (North American Province: n.p., 1951), p. 237.
3. Adapted from a pamphlet of the Apostolate of Christian Action, P.O. Box 24, Fresno, California.
4. The Maryknoll Fathers with the collaboration of Charles J. Callan, O.P., eds., *Daily Missal of the Mystical Body* (New York: Kenedy & Sons, 1961), p. 616.
5. Adapted from "Prayer to Saint Raphael," available at: www.columbia.edu.
6. Adapted from *St. Joseph Daily Missal*, rev. ed. (New York: Catholic Book, 1959), pp. 1107–1109.
7. Available at: www.2heartsnetwork.org.
8. Adapted from "Prayer to St. Gabriel, the Archangel," available at: www.catholicculture.org.
9. Adapted from *St. Joseph Daily Missal*, pp. 828–830.

10. *St. Joseph Daily Missal*, p. 1233.
11. Cardinal John Henry Newman, *Verses on Various Occasions* (London: Longmans, Green, 1890), pp. 300–302.
12. James Russell Lowell, *Last Poems of James Russell Lowell* (Boston: Houghton, Mifflin, 1895), pp. 24–26.
13. Trierer Gesangbuch, "O Holy Angel," *St. Rose Hymnal* (Boston: Mc Laughlin & Reilly, 1939), p. 151.
14. M. Caswell, "Sweet Angel of Mercy," *St. Rose Hymnal,* pp. 151–152.
15. From *A Treasury of Catholic Song* (Hagerstown, Md.: St. Mary's Auxiliary, 1915), pp. 182–183.